Time
FOR ALL THAT'S IMPORTANT

How to keep your life in balance when you can't tell which end is up.

TAMYRA HORST

Pacific Press® Publishing Association
Nampa, Idaho
Oshawa, Ontario, Canada

Edited by B. Russell Holt
Designed by Michelle C. Petz
Cover illustration by Bill Farnsworth © 1999 Stock Illustration
Source

Copyright © 2000 by
Pacific Press® Publishing Association
Printed in the United States of America
All Rights Reserved

ISBN 0-8163-1783-6

00 01 02 03 04 • 5 4 3 2 1

DEDICATION

Dedicated to God,
who balances my sin with His grace,
my restlessness and activity with His peace,
my discouragement with His hope,
my fears with His courage,
and my weakness with His strength,
and who never gives up on me
no matter how out of balance I become.

CONTENTS

INTRODUCTION

When one of my friends heard that I was working on a book about finding balance in life, she commented, "I give you credit for attempting it, but I don't think I could ever write credibly about that subject. I haven't found balance yet; I'm not sure I ever will."

Well, I definitely have the credibility of knowing what it's like to have a life out of balance! I have perfected the habit of taking on too much, trying to do more than I have time for and expecting it to all get done on time and just right. Yet in the midst of it all, I knew I was out of balance. I knew that the very things that were most important to me—my relationship with God, my husband Tim, my boys, other people, the things I felt God had asked me to do—were all too often pushed aside by the urgent, those things that screamed for immediate attention. I was always rushing, with a chronic sense of being behind.

Do I have credibility when writing about how to find balance? Have I arrived at the point where my life is totally balanced? Always?

I can write with credibility about searching for balance. Of coming to God and asking to be taught. For me, finding balance has been more of a process than an end result. God has taught me so much. There are still days that I'm rushing. But God has taught me to focus on what is truly important. He's shown me how to let go and say No—regardless of what anyone else thinks. I'm growing. Changing. Taking the time to do the things I want to do. Playing. Laughing. Relaxing. And not feeling guilty.

In this book, I'm sharing my journey—the things God has taught me about finding balance. While my life will always be busy, even hectic at times, God has shown me how to be busy doing what He desires me to do. More importantly, He's teaching me how to be the "me" He desires me to be.

—Tamyra Horst

CHAPTER ONE

Just a Skit

It was supposed to be only a skit, a simple illustration for family worship at camp meeting. Six children volunteered to participate. All I had to do was stand on the stage pretending to spin plates on sticks—like a juggler. In one hand, I held three sticks. As each child walked past me, he or she showed the audience, and then me, a poster depicting a role or responsibility—Pathfinder leader, cooking healthy meals, Bible study, mom, exercise, gardening, etc. When the child offered me this new role, I'd say Yes. Then he would hand me something associated with that role—a doll, a Bible, a pan, a hoe—and put another plate on my sticks, give it a spin, and walk off. I'd be left spinning another plate on the sticks in one hand and trying to hold all the accessories in the other. Until finally, I couldn't hold another thing—literally.

As the last child walked off, I dropped everything except the

Bible and read a verse. For the rest of the week, kids would pass me and say, "Hey, there's the lady that dropped everything!" Women would stop me and say, "That was too real!" or "That's my life!"

It was supposed to be only a skit, but it was very real. It was too much like our lives, too much like my life. Juggling so many roles and responsibilities, with more given to us constantly, we feel like we're going to drop it all. We always have a sense of being behind, of having to rush. We just can't keep up. But we don't know what else to do, except to keep on struggling.

Marcy works full-time outside the home—and inside the home. Her husband doesn't help much with the housework or the kids. Between juggling work and home, Marcy attempts to fit in a Bible study one evening a week and a weight management class another evening. Plus, she teaches Cradle Roll at her church. "I want to be involved at church, and I need the Bible study and weight management for myself," she says. "But when I walk in the house at the end of the day and the kids are fighting, the wash is piling up, and I can write my name in the dust on the furniture, I just feel like screaming."

Ashlin doesn't have children. Her husband and she have divided the housework in half. "We haven't gotten involved in church or our community much," she admits. "There is so much we want to do right now while we're young." She and her husband spend a lot of time playing. Hiking. Canoeing. Rock climbing. Biking. Traveling. They're always going somewhere or doing something. "Sometimes I think it might be nice to stay home one weekend and just work around the house or something. Or take the time to build a friendship with one of the women at church," Ashlin says. "But there is so much to do. We say we're going to stay home and get involved at church, but then there is another mountain to climb or a new bike path to try out."

When her oldest daughter was born, Steffany chose to quit her job and stay home with her children. "At first life was a fog. Never getting enough sleep. Always being tired. I felt that I was accomplishing something just to take a shower and get dinner ready by the time Neal got home. But then as the kids got older, people tended to ask me to do things because they thought I had all this time. I was at home. I didn't work. Even I forgot that my priority should be to play with, teach, and just be with my kids. Some days I just can't keep up with all the demands." Steffany serves as room mother for two of her children at school. There are field trips and fundraisers to organize and cupcakes to bake. At church, she teaches the juniors and organizes the fellowship meals. "And someone is always wanting me to baby-sit since I'm already home," she adds. "How can I say No?"

My own life tends to get out of balance easily. I have good intentions. Now that the boys are both in school during the day, Tim and I have chosen for me to remain at home in order to write and serve the ministries in which I'm involved. But too often my days are so full of other things that writing gets put off—not just for days, but for weeks and months. My list of things to do for the ministries grows longer and longer while I take care of the urgent requests that pop up each day—until the to do list seems overwhelming, and I put it off because I doubt that I can ever get caught up.

No matter how much we're asked to do, we continue on. We struggle to find balance. To juggle everything without dropping any of it. We try to find ways to juggle fewer things. We try time management ideas. We try to learn to be more organized. And it helps some. Still there is always more that needs to be done. And we find ourselves barely able to keep our heads above water.

But I don't want just to get everything done. Just to manage somehow to keep up with all my responsibilities. I don't want just to make it through each day, accomplishing the urgent, falling into bed exhausted at the end of the day. I don't believe that is what God wants for me. Or for you. I believe He's promised us more—rest, joy, an abundant life.

But too often life gets out of hand. The demands become too many. Rest and joy are non-existent, and the only thing that is abundant is the list of things to do.

Recently I sent a card to a friend that pretty much sums up the problem. It said, "We wouldn't have so many bad hair days if we weren't wearing so many hats." Too many hats. Too many roles. Wife. Mom. Daughter. Friend. Employee. Church worker. Volunteer. Housekeeper. Taxi driver. Nurse. Encourager. Cook. The list goes on and on.

And each of those roles carries so many responsibilities. As a mom, it's hard to keep up with cooking, cleaning, shopping, homework, getting kids to school, to soccer, and to a myriad of other places, plus teach them about strangers, sex, dating, God, and how to ride a two-wheeler. On top of all that, what our kids really want is for us to spend time with them. Playing. Talking. Snuggling.

It's a full-time, important job. And that's just one role! Add to that all you need to do at work, church, and in the community, plus the time you need to give to other family members and friends, and it's no wonder so many of us feel that we're constantly running and constantly tired.

I know. This has been my life. Just trying to keep up with the things that *had* to be done each day took all my time. Many important things fell by the wayside. I was forgetting things. Losing things. And feeling guilty for all the stuff I wasn't doing—or was doing, but not as well as I could. I got on the plane in tears the day my youngest son kissed me good-bye at the airport again and said, "When you come home this time, Mommy, can you stay awhile?" (Later I found out that his concern wasn't due so much to the fact that I had been gone a lot, but to the fact that when I was gone, his dad kept him busy working!)

I knew something had to give. But what? All the things I was doing were good things. Most were things I felt sure God had called me to do. But I knew in my heart that the things in my life weren't in the right order. Too many days I was too tired from all the good things I was doing to get up and have time with God. I had quit my job when my oldest son was born to stay home and raise my children. But I was putting in enough volunteer hours to be working a full-time job. And the boys were spending most of their time playing by themselves while I tried to keep up with everything. That's not what I had intended. It's not what I wanted. Was that how life was going to be no matter what?

Somewhere there had to be a balance between "doing" and "being." There had to be a way to work, raise a family, *and* enjoy life, too.

I wanted time to play with my boys, to talk with them. Josh is a teenager now. So many changes. So many challenges. I know how critical the teen years are, and I want to be there for him. To keep the doors of communication open. To be involved in his life as much as he will allow. To guide him through the tough stuff that I know lies ahead. I believe that it's more important for me to be here for him now than at almost any other point in his life.

I needed time to spend with friends—not always working on a project together, but just having fun and talking. But it seemed that the only time I got together with friends was to work on some church or school project. When one of my closest friends moved out of state, it hit me that I hadn't taken the time to cultivate new friendships. Seldom did I call someone just to talk. Notes and phone calls of encouragement were few and far between—yet that's how my ministry had begun. And many people were afraid to call me because I was so busy. They didn't want to interrupt all the "important things" I was doing. How could I have friends or encourage others if I didn't have time for people?

Then there was Tim and family. Tim and I had made a commitment to "date" once a month. But it had been months since we had had any time to ourselves, since just the two of us had gone out together. Days slipped by easily without meaningful conversation. Nights found us both falling exhaustedly to sleep, barely able to say good night. And the only time I saw my family was on holidays. Weeks would go by without time to stop by my mom's house, and she lived only ten minutes away! Weren't people more important than things accomplished?

At the same time, I loved most of what I was doing. I loved writing and traveling and speaking. I loved meeting all the new people and seeing God work in incredible ways. I loved my involvement in women's ministries at the conference and union levels. These were all things I felt God had called me to do. They hadn't been things I had ever dreamed of doing. Yet God had dreamt them for me. And I enjoyed it all. But still, the appointments were coming more frequently. And I was always planning some new idea or project.

And I still wanted to be involved in my local church. I loved the dozen or so kids in the junior-earliteen class I taught. I enjoyed working on all the church committees and teams; each held a special place in my heart. But I knew I wasn't doing any of these things as well as I should. Too many things were going undone. Too many details were falling by the wayside. But what should I quit doing?

Besides, I was growing older. And heavier. Where was the time to eat right and exercise? Wasn't I supposed to be taking care of my body, too? I couldn't get up any earlier or go to bed any later. Where was I supposed to fit it all in? In the busyness of the day, meals were too often whatever I could grab.

And of course, my time with God was supposed to be the most important part of my day. I was supposed to include Him throughout my day. I said He was my top priority, but too often the way I spent my time showed that my real priorities were deadlines and getting things done. Too many mornings I overslept and hit the floor running—skipping time with God, skipping breakfast, and flying through the day without much thought about it.

I had come to a place of exhaustion. I was tired of running.

Tired of feeling guilty because I couldn't keep up with everything. I felt that I had nothing left to give. Heading out for another weekend away from home, I desperately wanted to cancel. To call and say I couldn't come. That I didn't have anything left to share. There were several Sabbath mornings when getting ready for church took every ounce of effort I had. Just putting one foot in front of the other seemed to take every bit of my strength. I didn't want to go, and I didn't know why. It wasn't like me. I had always wanted to be at church—to be a part of things. But all the demands on my time were catching up with me. Something had to give.

I'd been here before. Attempting to slow down. To simplify my life. To cut things out. To say No. I had learned a lot in every one of those areas. Yet the results weren't lasting. I'd do fine for awhile, but before I knew it, I'd be overwhelmed, overworked, and over-tired. How could I find lasting balance? How could I find time for what was really important? How could I do all I needed to do, all I *should* do, and still find time to be me?

I knew where to find the answer. It was just like the skit had said—I needed to drop everything and turn to God. "So teach *us* to number our days, That we may gain a heart of wisdom" (Psalm 90:12, NKJV).

Yes, Lord!

Thinking and Talking About It

1. What is your schedule like? Comfortable? Too hectic? Over-demanding?

2. Make a list of all your roles—including employment, church

committees and responsibilities, volunteer activities, roles involving family and friends, etc.

3. List all your roles in order of priority to you.

4. If you could spend an afternoon doing anything you like, what would it be? What would it take to make that happen?

CHAPTER TWO

How Did We Get Here?

There was a time when life was simpler. Families ate supper together—even breakfast together—sitting around the table talking and laughing. There was time for a Sunday drive—a leisurely drive—through the country, taking time to look at the farms and fields and flower gardens. I remember driving around at Christmas time just to look at the lights on people's houses. (Does that give away my age?) There was a time when people sat on the front porch swing and talked to the neighbors while sipping tall glasses of lemonade. Such a time sounds simple and peaceful—and impossible. A nice dream.

Today a lot of us don't even know our neighbors. And there is no time to sit. Or to leisurely drive anywhere. Everywhere we go, we're rushing. We go only where we have to go. Family meals together are few and far between in most homes. Meals are quick and eaten on the run or in front of the TV. There are too many things to do. So we look at the Christmas lights while we rush to do our last-minute shopping in malls so crowded with irritable people that we move along being pushed by the crowd.

You'd think that we would have more time today. Just think of all the things that have been added to our homes to make life easier. Dishwashers. Washing machines and dryers. Microwaves. Instant meals—just heat and serve. Gone are the days of putting clothes through wringer washers. Of spending hours ironing. Cooking meals from scratch. Scrubbing floors and walls on hands and knees with scouring pads. Few people today plant a garden and then harvest the vegetables, canning or freezing them for winter. I remember my mom's huge garden and the shelves of shiny glass jars full of a summer's work. There are a few things in our cupboards that I've canned, but most of what it holds has been bought at the "bent and banged" grocery store down the road.

Life is more convenient outside our homes as well as inside. Our cars go faster. We can catch a plane and be across the country in just a few hours. Computers have opened a whole new world of convenience—e-mail, online shopping, research on any topic with just a click or two. I love it that I can "talk" to my friend, Tanya, in another state almost everyday just like when she lived only ten minutes away.

Even at work technology has added lots of machines to make the job simpler. No more carbon paper—we have photocopiers instead. Need something somewhere instantly? Fax it. Automated machines do the work once done by hand. My boys and I sometimes stop by a local pretzel factory and take the tour. The displays show how at one time the pretzels had to be twisted by hand. Today, machines twist more pretzels in an hour than human fingers could twist in a day.

Technology is supposed to make all the jobs we do simpler and less time consuming. So you would think we'd have more time. But instead we just fill our time with more and more things to do. I've often thought and heard others say, "If only I had a few more hours in the day . . . ." But in my heart I know that I would just fill those hours, too. And still need more!

But why? Why do we long for time to relax and play, yet fill our days with more and more to do? Why do we fill our lives so full that there is no time left? In his book, *Margin*, Dr. Richard Swenson describes our lives today as marginless. Margin is that extra room at the side of a piece of a paper. It's a place to add what you've forgotten. A place to put a little extra. But today our lives have no margins. No place to add a little extra. No place to put what we've forgotten to write in our schedules. Nowhere to squeeze in a few minutes with a friend who drops by or calls unexpectedly. Our lives are completely full. We need a margin. A little unscheduled time for those unexpected things that pop up. Or those fun things you wish you could do on the spur of a moment. Or a moment just to sit and watch or listen or read or close your eyes and dream.

Why do we long for those moments of margin, yet pack our lives so full?

For each of us the reasons may be slightly different. But there are some basic answers I've seen in my own life and in the lives of others.

1. People applaud those who are busy and accomplish a lot. Friends say, "Wow! I don't know how you do it all! I wish I could accomplish half of what you do." We admire busy people. We equate busyness with value. Without even realizing it, we're telling people that to be really valuable they have to accomplish things. And the more things they accomplish, the more valuable they are. The person who puts in the most hours and has the highest production figures is the most valued employee at work. The person who volunteers the most hours for the most organizations is rewarded with awards and recognition from the community.

It's true in the church, too. We applaud those who serve on numerous committees and attend all the socials and potlucks—not just attending, but helping and being a part of everything that happens. We applaud them and then ask them to do more. The same person may hold several leadership positions though each position could be a full-time job in itself. Instead of holding each other accountable to be a good steward of time, we encourage each other to take on more and then applaud those who do the most. Instead of helping people to be responsible and enabling them to have time for all the important things in their lives, we ask them to take on more than they should be doing—especially people who seem capable and accomplish a lot with little obvious effort.

"It's hard to quit. To say, 'I can't do this any longer!' when everyone is saying, 'I really admire all you're doing. No one can do it quite like you do,'" sighs Brittany, "Just this week I received an e-mail from a friend telling me in one sentence that I needed to slow down and then in the next telling me how much she admired all I did. I want to quit; I want to slow down, but I don't want to let anyone down. I don't want people to think I can't handle it. I guess, honestly, I like it that they admire me and applaud what I do. I don't want that to stop. Would they still like me if I weren't doing all I'm doing?"

The applause of people cheers us on. We keep going, keep running, even when we feel we can't go another step. We don't want the applause to stop. We're afraid that if we stop, it will stop, too. That leads us to the next reason we fall into the trap of overdoing.

2. Doing things gives us a sense of value and purpose. When we hear the applause of others, it tells us, "You're valuable. You're worth something." That may not be what people are really saying, but many times it's what we're hearing. Even as children we learn that what we do gets us attention more often than anything else. Shelley found herself caught up in the having-to-accomplish-something-to-feel-good-about-myself syndrome. "I grew up in a big family," she recalls. "It was easy to get lost in the crowd. You were noticed when you did something, accomplished something. That is when you heard words of praise. I learned early on that to be noticed you had to do something bigger and better than everyone else."

But it's more than the applause. It's being able to say that we've done something, that we've accomplished something. We feel good at the end of the day when we can list a number of things that we got done. And the longer the list, the better we feel about ourselves. At times, I've not only crossed things off my to do list, but I've even added things that weren't on the list and then crossed them off so that my list would look even better! Being able to do things gives us a sense of purpose.

When I quit my job to stay home with my son, I hated the question, "So, what do you do?" A stay-at-home mom didn't sound important even though I had told myself that it was the most important role in my life. But at the end of the day, what did I have to show for my time? A toy-strewn house? The things I did each day would need to be done again tomorrow. I was judging what was important by society's standards. I believed others felt that being a stay-at-home mom wasn't an important role. That I should be working. Producing. Bringing in an income. Sometimes I still struggle with these feelings.

Most of what I do is volunteer work, ministering to people I will never meet (through writing) or people I'll never see again (through speaking). How do I know if what I've done has had an impact on someone's life? How do I know if I've accomplished anything? Being paid for what we do gives us a sense of accomplishment. We're rewarded for what we've done. But being a mom or a wife or a friend or ministering to others often doesn't have tangible rewards. Many times, I believe, we won't truly know what we've accomplished until we can see it through God's eyes.

Yet outward appearance and awards are important to us. We judge how valuable we are as an employee by how much work we do and how many hours we put in and how well we are remunerated for our work. Often we choose our church leaders more by how much they do than by what is truly in their hearts. We even decide how good a Christian someone is by outward evidences. Stacy Rinehart writes in *Upside Down*, "During a seminar, I once asked,

'How would you define the ideal Christian?' I was amazed at how quickly people responded, speaking in terms of one's devotional life, evangelism habits, monetary giving patterns, church involvement, and family life. From group to group, as I've asked that question, I've received strikingly similar responses."

We forget that it's easy "to do things." It's easy to look good on the outside. Outward evidences give us something we can see and measure. But they're not always accurate. We forget that salvation is a free gift because of Whose we are, not because of what we do. We can't do anything to earn salvation. We can't do anything to make us more valuable—at least not to God. But we forget, and push on, trying hard to please, to be someone.

3. Having things requires a price—literally. Someone has to pay for all the things we have and all the things we do. In his business, my husband works with a lot of new housing developments. In doing so, he has seen a growing trend. No longer are most homes simple family dwellings—three bedrooms, two car garage, living room, dining room, and kitchen. Houses, today, are huge! Three-car garages are the standard. Every room has outlets for phone and cable TV. New cars, today, cost what homes used to cost. And today's lifestyle costs more. Daycare. Convenience foods. People are eating out several nights a week. Andy Dappen writes in an article for *Reader's Digest* (August 1999, p. 136), "In the early 1970s, 26 percent of household food money was spent on meals away from home; today that figure is 40 percent." All the activities our children—and their parents—are involved in cost money. We have to work more to pay for all we have. The more we do, the more life costs. So we work more to earn more so we can do more and have more. But do we need it all?

4. We don't realize that we don't have to do it all. Busyness is the norm. Everyone is busy, stressed out, and tired. Hospitals and churches offer stress management classes. Stress-related diseases are on the rise. Sometimes we just get caught up in all of it and don't realize that we have a choice. We can say No. We can choose to stay home, put up our feet, and read a book.

"All the other moms were taking their kids to soccer, gymnastics, and the youth Bible study," Melinda says. "It was like a joke when we all sat around watching a game or practice. We laughed about being nothing more than taxi drivers. But inside I wasn't laughing. I was tired of getting off work and having to pick up the kids, pull up to the drive-through for supper, and head to another practice or game or meeting. I just wanted to go home. But I thought that was what all good moms did." Melinda softly laughed as she continued, "Then one night Joe said, 'You know, you don't have to do this. The kids will survive just fine without being involved in everything.' I thought about what he said and realized that he was right. I wanted the kids to be involved in some things. I knew that students who are involved in activities do better and get into less trouble. But maybe my kids didn't have to do *everything!* That was a changing point. From then on, the kids chose one thing to be a part of— something that really mattered to them. Funny! Not only did life get easier for me, but even the kids seemed to enjoy the slower schedule."

"My kids are grown," Rebekah says, "and I retired from my job six years ago. I thought that life would slow down. But if anything, I'm busier than ever—babysitting grandchildren, volunteering at the community center and the Humane League, and helping with things at church." Rebekah and her husband have lived in the same small town all their lives. They've watched life change and get busier. "I always thought our retirement years would be quiet—sitting on the porch, traveling with friends, finally getting time to work on my flower beds." She laughs. "But my flower beds are still full of weeds. Do I have a choice? I don't know. I never thought about it. If I don't do it, who will?"

Most of us don't think about having a choice. We get caught up doing. People ask. We say Yes—not realizing that it's up to us to stop it. Most of the time we don't even stop to ask God, "What do You want me to do?"

5. Our real priorities are often not what we say they are. Not down in the core of our hearts. We want them to be. We say they are. But our actions show that they're not. We say that God is the top priority of our lives, but we rush through our day without spending time with Him. We say that family is important to us, but we get so busy that we don't have time to sit down for a dinner together, to have family worship, or to talk about the things that are really important to us. We want to get involved in church, but we put in late hours at work and don't have time.

It's a subtle problem and one that we often don't even realize. But deep down inside, the drive to do things keeps us busy. We may not think about it, but we find value and purpose in doing, not in being. If you ask someone to tell you about himself, usually he will tell you what he does—his job, his hobbies. He won't really tell you about himself—who he is, what he is about. So we keep doing. Keep rushing around. Keep taking on more. Keep working more. Keep giving more and more. We want life to be different. We want to laugh more. Play more. Pray more. We talk about our priorities, but we rarely change our lives and let our priorities determine what we do and how we spend our time.

We've become overly busy, stressed out, burned out, and tired. But we like the applause. We find our value and purpose in it. We don't realize that we can stop. We believe we have to keep going to keep up with all the things we want or have. We want it to be different. But where do we go from here? How do we find balance with all that we're asked to do or need to do?

Thinking and Talking About It

1. What would you list as the most important things in your life—your top priorities?

2. Write out your schedule for a week, listing everything that you need to do or plan to do. Include things that may not be part of your usual written schedule but nevertheless are things you typically do, such as cleaning house, fixing meals, quiet time, playing, etc.

3. Write your priorities at the top of a piece of paper in columns. Now take your schedule and list all the entries under the appropriate column.

4. What does your schedule show about your priorities?

CHAPTER THREE

Where Do We Go From Here?

For a long time, I didn't want to admit that my life was out of balance. I liked the thought that I could do it all. Keep it all together. Meet all the demands. I didn't want to admit that I was overwhelmed and exhausted. I kept thinking, "Once I get past this or that, life will slow down." But it didn't. Every time I finished one big project, another had already replaced it. The more you take on, the more people will ask you to do. So I took on more and more without letting anything go.

But finally there was no denying it. I just couldn't keep up. I was dropping things. Worn out, used up, with nothing left to give, I had to admit that I was over scheduled and out of balance.

God never intended for us to live an over-committed life. He wants our lives to be balanced. He promises rest, not overwhelmedness. Peace, not stress. He invites us, " 'Come to me, all you who are weary and burdened, and I will give you rest. Take my yoke upon you and learn from me, for I am gentle and humble in heart, and you will find rest for your souls. For my yoke is easy and my burden is light' " (Matthew 11:28-30, NIV). David Henderson paraphrases Jesus' words like this: "Come to Me, all you who are worn out and weighed down by scrambling to meet the demands of others, and I will bring quiet to your spirits. Serve *Me*, follow *Me*, and—because I am caring and understanding—I will stop the clamoring in your souls. For what I ask of you is not a burden at all" (*Discipleship Journal*, Jan/Feb 97, p. 52). God never planned for us to feel burdened and exhausted. Mr. Henderson suggests that we tend to struggle under different yokes—heavier yokes—than Jesus intended for us. "And almost always, when we look closely at the initials carved in the burden that we strain against, we find that they are yokes of our own making" (Ibid.).

I know that is true in my life. I take on so many things without thinking to ask, "Is this what God wants me to do?" Or even considering how this new activity will affect my schedule or my life. How it will fit into God's plan in my life.

How do I change? How do we begin to find balance?

First, we must realize—and admit—that our lives are out of control and that we need balance. That we just can't do it all. We have to accept that God doesn't want us to be overburdened and exhausted. That something has to change.

We must want to change. Be willing to change. It will take effort. We have to change the way we look at life and take time to think differently. God created us to be human *beings*, not human *doings*.

Here are six things we can "be" to help us be balanced:

1. Be real. Be who God intends you to be. He created you for a purpose. Jeremiah 29:11 tells us that God has plans for us—plans for peace and hope and a future. Peace, not stress. Hope, not despair. He created each of us to fit a particular part of His plan.

Begin by taking stock of who you are and what God has created you to be. Ask questions such as, What is my real purpose? What does God want me to accomplish in my life? Why am I doing what I'm doing? Is this what God wants for me? What are my priorities? My goals? What are the gifts and talents that God has given me? If you're not sure what your gifts and talents are, ask your pastor for a spiritual-gifts test. Ask close friends what talents they see in you. Think about what you enjoy doing the most.

As I look at my life, I know that to me, the most important thing is being the daughter of God that He desires me to be. I want to be totally and completely His. I want my life to be lived His way. His plans for me are the best because He loves me completely, and His desires for me will make me the best I can be. I want His hopes and dreams. I want to live a life submitted totally to Him.

But I fall short. I get so busy doing things—usually good things "for" Him—that I don't have time "with" Him. Busyness is one of the devil's best tools. He wants to keep us so busy that we don't have time for what really matters. He wants us so caught up in the moment that we forget about what life is really all about. God didn't create us for today, but for eternity. His plans, His hopes, His desires for us are all based on eternity. We need to concentrate not just on making it through the day but on living for eternity. This life is temporary. It's a preparation for our real future. The devil wants us so busy making a life for ourselves here, that we don't even think about our life in eternity. He wants us so focused on making this life the good life, that we forget how temporary some things are and lose sight of what's truly important. God has so much more for us.

I'd like my life to be described the way author Beth Moore's bio line describes hers: "Her life is full of activity, but one commitment remains constant: counting all things but loss for the excellence of knowing Christ Jesus, the Lord" (*A Woman's Heart: God's Dwelling Place,* p. 4). I know my life will always be busy. I know that, for me, finding balance doesn't mean lazy days. I love activity. But I want the activity to be a result of my relationship with God. I want all I do to be because of Him and His call on my life. He is most important to me. I can trust that my life will be balanced if I'm doing what He wants. I know that He wants that kind of life for me—not the chaotic stress so normal to my days but rest and purpose in the busyness.

What is my purpose? To be who God intends me to be. Through us, God desires to make a difference in our sphere of the world; to draw others to Him through our relationship with Him. He uses all that happens to us, and all that we do, to help us experience Him more. His purpose for our lives is for us to know Him as intimately as a human being can know God.

What do I want to accomplish? Only what He desires. Nothing more. Nothing less. Which leads to the question: "Why am I doing what I'm doing?"

Look at what you're doing in your life. Why are you doing it?

Does it match God's plan for you? Or are you doing it because someone else expects you to do it or wants you to? Is it because you don't want to disappoint anyone? I have to admit, there were things in my life (maybe there still are) that I was doing not because God wanted me to but because people expected me to do them. Or because I wanted to earn money. (We all need money and must work to earn it, but sometimes we work too much for the wrong reason. God will provide.) At times I've done things because they gave me a sense of value; because I wanted a title and recognition. And sometimes I've done things because if I didn't do them, who else would?

None of these are terrible reasons for doing something, but they are not the right reason. I want to do things because they are part of God's plan for my life.

What are my priorities? For each of us, the answers will be different. And the answers will change through out our lives. So it's good to take stock from time to time and decide what's important. In my own life, I've decided that God comes first, then my family. Tim and the boys are the most important part of my life on this earth. Unfortunately, my schedule hasn't always reflected that fact, but it's changing. I want to keep my relationship with Tim strong and healthy. I love him. I want that love to grow. And that can happen only as we continually build our relationship together by spending time with each other. Talking. Sharing. Keeping that connection.

My sons, Joshua and Zachary, are the joys of my life. I smile just thinking about them. The twinkle in Josh's eyes when he smiles.

His sense of humor. Zack's dimples and creativeness. They are growing so fast. Josh is already a teenager. This last year, he's grown taller than either his dad or I. I've watched him this summer and am amazed at the young man he is becoming. Where did my little "buddy" go? Was there really a day when I could carry him? When he could fit on my lap? I don't want to miss out on a moment of my time with them. I want us to enjoy each other. To play. To pray. I want to really know my boys. To be a part of their lives. To know their struggles and be able to talk together about them. To guide them. I want my family to come before anything else. Most things are so much more temporary than we realize. Our homes will be left behind. So will all the material things we fill them with. The only things we can take with us to heaven are the people in our lives.

After family, the priorities in my life include friends and the ministry to which God has called me. Currently, that ministry is writing and women's ministries. That is where my passion is. Everything I learn and experience, I begin to "write" about in my head. I want to share it with other women. I want others to experience the value and confidence and unconditional love I've found in God.

At a leadership seminar, a pastor friend was challenged to choose the three most important areas of his life and to focus on them. Focusing on the most important things in our lives helps to keep us from being over-committed. For me, the top three things in my life are (1) my relationship with God; (2) my family; and (3) my friends and ministry (maybe that's really four things!). These are the areas I'm attempting to focus on in my life. I often remind myself of these priorities. When I'm asked to do something new, I consider it in the light of these commitments. How will this activity affect my time with God? What about my family? Will it fit in with the ministry that I'm already doing? Will I still have time for people? To write notes? Make phone calls? Visit?

I've made a list of all my "jobs" and put them in the order of priority in my life. There are more than three areas of my life that are important—for example, taking care of myself, being active in my local church and in my sons' school, keeping my home neat and organized, fixing healthful meals for my family. I pray over this list each week, asking God to show me what needs to be top priority and what needs to go.

You'll notice that I haven't listed a job as one of my priorities. Currently, I consider my job part of the ministry I'm involved in— writing, speaking, and women's ministries. It encompasses a lot. But it's not a regular nine-to-five job. A job may be something you have to do and commit time; it may not be something you choose to focus on. God may have you involved in this job because of the people you can influence or because of what you're learning. I believe God uses all aspects of our lives to teach us. But sometimes, we put too much focus on our jobs, allowing them to prevent us from being involved in anything else.

Tim's job is important to him. But when he comes home, the job is left behind. It's time to focus on other things. His job is not one of the top three most important areas of his life—more like four or five. Yet he is a very responsible and committed employee. Putting in more hours than he has to, working meticulously and thoroughly. That's his personality. But his job is not his top priority. One of the priorities in his life right now is our home. He's in the middle of a huge construction project here. The house hasn't been a priority before. But it seemed the timing was right, and after prayer and consideration, he believed it was the way God was leading. So the house has become one of his top three priorities. One of Tim's gifts is teaching. He loves sharing the Bible. At work, he's been sharing the Bible with one of his co-workers. That's something important to him, too.

Your job may be one of your top three priorities. Or it may be four or five on your list—something you need to do, but not the most important thing. Housework is like that for me. It's important to me to have a clean and orderly home. Disorder and clutter drive me crazy. But cleaning is not one of the most important things to me (although it's definitely in my top ten). There have been days when I've skipped cleaning because something more important came up. (OK, I usually try to squeeze cleaning in somewhere, but I'm learning to put the truly important things first!)

That's what happened the other week. I didn't know when I was going to get a chance to clean. I was meeting a writing deadline, and I had speaking appointments on Friday and Sabbath. Normally, I clean on Fridays. But since Josh was at camp, I had promised to spend a day with Zack doing whatever he wanted—a date-with-mom day. Each summer I set aside a little extra money to do things with the boys. That week, the only day that worked was Thursday. The day I *should* have been cleaning. But the boys are top priority, so I skipped cleaning and went go-carting, then to lunch, and finally, to the Humane Society to look at dogs. Zack and I had a great time. The cleaning got done on Monday. And we even invited visitors home for lunch after I spoke at my home church on Sabbath—with a house that hadn't been cleaned nor food prepared. But we had an impromptu meal and a great visit! I felt good knowing that I had done what was most important.

While driving somewhere one day, I heard a quote on a radio program. It said something like this: "Christians today don't accomplish much because they are trying to do too much. They need to focus on what God has called them to do and let everything else go." We try to carry too big a load, to do too much. In *Upside Down: The Paradox of Christian Leadership,* Stacy Rinehart suggests that God has given each of us gifts and talents for a specific part of His work. We run into trouble when we attempt to do more than what God has called us to do. Not only do we burn out, but we get in the way of someone else doing what God wants them to do. What has God called you to do? Stick to it.

Be real. Be the real you—the you that God has created you to be. Maybe you aren't sure who that is. Maybe you have wondered if God even cares. He does. His Word tells us that He does. We're reminded by Scripture that He has a plan for our lives. He knew that plan when He created us. He has given us gifts and talents and a part to play in His kingdom. Believe it! Live it!

2. Be radical. Be willing to go against the flow. To say No. To judge yourself through God's standards, not society's. The world tells us that we need big houses, fancy cars, and expensive clothes. It tells us that we need to work, work, work. That we need titles and positions. That our kids need to be involved in lots of activities. God tells us that the most important thing we can do is to love Him and to love others. We're to encourage one another and build each other up.

Unfortunately, that's not what this world is all about. On a recent morning news/talk program, one of the anchors said that she was surprised when people were kind. That she's grown to expect people to be mean, rude, and unfriendly. I knew what she was talking about. A friend and I had traveled to Georgia to speak at a leadership conference. At the airport we rented a car and headed toward the camp about an hour away. Half way there, we were rear-ended. When I got out of the car, I expected the driver of the other car to be angry. To make excuses. But he didn't. He was concerned that we might have been hurt. He readily admitted that the accident was his fault. I had stopped for the traffic light; he didn't. The closest building was a bank, so I went there to find a phone. A teller offered me a phone on one of the desks that wasn't being used. A customer waiting in line offered to make the phone call for me when she realized that I didn't know the name of the road or cross roads I was on. The police officer was nice. I had expected him to be abrupt. He took the report and told me where I could go to get the exhaust pipe temporarily hooked back up. The man at the service station fixed it for free. That night when I spoke, I began by saying that I had just been in the nicest accident I'd ever been in. It surprised me how nice everyone was. It's sad when we expect people to be rude and unfriendly. When we're used to our neighbors not looking up when we walk past.

God calls us to something different. Not just to be nice but to realize that we can't always measure true success by outward accomplishments. Society encourages us to have a list of things we've done to show that we've accomplished something. At the end of our lives, an obituary column will list all our "accomplishments" in the way of jobs and positions we've held. At high school reunions, many of us are given books telling what our classmates have "accomplished" in the years since graduation. But God measures accomplishments differently than society. At the end of the day, the stay-at-home mom may not have crossed off significant things from her to-do list. But she may have played with her children, laughing with them, encouraging them, pointing them to Jesus through her actions, love, and prayers. To God, that's an accomplishment.

At work, your boss might see that you've finished the project you were working on for him. But the accomplishment God sees is the smile you gave the secretary, the way you listened to your co-worker pour out her heart, the prayers you sent up for each of the people you met. At church, your Sabbath School class may appreciate your teaching or your class comments. But your real accomplishment might have been stooping down and talking to those kids from the kindergarten class. Or sitting with the single parent and helping her with her children. Or giving a hug to that person you barely know who just looked like he could use one.

Being radical means being willing to trust God and to follow His leading—not the world's expectations. Your list of accomplishments on this planet may not seem long, but the list in heaven will be based on entirely different criteria.

3. Be simple. I've often longed for simpler days. I've wished for summer days to just sit outside in a lawn chair with a cold drink and a good book. Or winter afternoons with a friend by the fire. But life is far from simple. There are too many deadlines. Too many meetings. Too many appointments. Too many expectations.

How do we live more simple lives in such a fast-paced, demanding world?

Part of the answer comes from being radical. Being willing *not* to live up to today's expectations. Trade in the big house for a smaller house with smaller payments that can be more easily met. Skip buying a new car and make the old car last. Eat out less and spend more time as a family around the dinner table. Turn off the TV and play games or read books together. Instead of having to have it all, buy only what you can afford. Do it yourself when you can, instead of hiring someone else to do it.

Our true treasures are in heaven, not on this earth. We need to seek God's will in the things we buy and own. Does God want us to have incredible debt and lifestyles that require us to work long hours without time for much else? Larry Burkett's *Money Matters* newsletter (June 1999) gave the following statistics:

Americans watch more than fifty hours of television a week, yet devote less than five hours volunteering. We're now working more than forty-seven hours each week, while spending only seventeen hours with our children. And it's estimated that we pay nearly ten percent of our income in interest, but give only two percent back to God. Consumer

debt is rising, and revolving credit card accounts now exceed
$500 billion. While our personal savings rate was at a record
low of minus 0.6 percent in March.

This is the norm in America. But is it what God wants?

Tim and I have tried to live differently. We bought a small,
older home with house payments that we could afford on Tim's
income alone. That gave me the freedom to stay home with the
boys. Our home for the last thirteen years has had five rooms—two
bedrooms, one bath, a kitchen, and a living room. There is a
basement with the laundry and Tim's workshop. This year, we're
adding a second level that will give us three bedrooms and a bath
upstairs. We'll turn the downstairs bedrooms into a dining room
and family room. We're able to afford the remodel by doing the
work ourselves with help from a few friends and from money we've
saved all these years.

Our cars aren't new. In fact, we've never owned a new car. We
eat out once or twice a month—usually on a date, sometimes as a
family. We don't own video games or a VCR. Our TV is a hand-me-
down. We'd rather go for a walk, play a game, or read books together
than watch TV. (Maybe the boys would rather watch TV, but they
enjoy doing things as a family, too.) We have one credit card and
charge only what we know we can pay off when the bill comes—
never carrying a balance. Tim automatically puts money into savings
every pay day. Instead of Disney World for a vacation, we pack our
sleeping bags and tent and head for campgrounds near mountains
and hiking trails. Fun doesn't have to cost a lot. One summer, the

kids enjoyed the time they spent with their dad building a tree house in the backyard. They've learned to appreciate nature instead of computer games—though, like all kids, they enjoy a game or two or three, given a chance.

Living simple means cutting back on activities, too. How many evenings a week are you willing to be gone from home? How many evenings *are* you gone? If the two don't match, look at what is taking up your evenings and decide what you can cut. Our kids don't have to be involved in every possible activity either. Begin now to teach them how to have balance in their lives when they're on their own. Let them each choose one activity to be involved in at a time. It will make their life, and yours, easier.

We can also choose more effectively *what* we're involved in. What is really important? What fits with your priorities? What has God called you to do? Be real. Do what God has planned for you. Let other things go. Remember that time is important. We're called to be good stewards of our time as well as our money.

4. Be firm. Joni Eareckson Tada has this to say:

A busy day doesn't fluster me as long as I make lots of lists and am strict about my priorities. And when the demands get rigorous, I just have to say, "Lord Jesus, I'm going to disappoint people. I'm going to miss deadlines. But I'll do the best I can with what energy You give." It's one way to keep guilt over unmet expectations from eating me up. That's the sin that turns your sense of joy in work into a tiring duty. And nothing sags the spirit more than doing things out of a dry sense of duty (*Discipleship Journal*, Jan/Feb 1997, p. 53).

Know your priorities and stick to them. Don't let people persuade you or pressure you. We're not here to please people. That is a tough concept for me to accept. I'm a world-class people pleaser. I want to make everyone happy and keep peace. I've spent my life striving to live up to everyone's expectations for me. I don't like letting people down or disappointing them. But I realize that as I've run myself ragged trying to please everyone around me, I've let God down by doing things He hasn't asked me to do—but had in mind for someone else. I've also let Him down by not doing, as well as I could, the things He *has* called me to do (and gifted me for)—because my energies were being spent somewhere else. We can't please everyone. We need to choose to please God.

Say No. Without guilt. Without excuses. If it's not what God wants, let it go. Say No to good things in order to say Yes to the best things—the things God desires for you. There are a lot of good things out there to do. We can get so busy doing the good things that we don't have time for the truly important things. Decide what is truly important to you and stick to it.

Realize the downside of not being firm and allowing your schedule to get out of balance.

It's more than the overload and over-tiredness. Our busy schedules affect how well we do all the things we try to do; they affect the people we love. One mom explains, "I was constantly on the phone or on the computer, and as a result, I was constantly getting mad at my kids. I knew it was time to give it up. For me, it was a matter of trusting God: Do I really believe that if I invest my time where God wants me to invest it—my family—He will bless my ministry?" (Elaine Minamide, "Overcommitted Moms: Workaholics at Home," *Focus on the Family,* February 1999).

Do you believe that if you do only what God desires that He will take care of the rest? How you live your life shows what you believe about God. Does your time, and how you spend it, show that you trust God? Do you trust Him enough to say No? Do you trust Him enough to depend on Him—rather than your accomplishments—for your sense of personal value and self-worth? Do you trust Him enough to believe that if it doesn't get done, it's not the end of the world? Are you willing to obey God instead of trying to keep up with the world?

5. *Be focused.* Christ was. That is how He could do all He did. He was focused on three things, as we see in John 13:3. "Jesus, knowing that the Father had given all things into His hands, and that He had come from God and was going to God . . ." (NIV).

First, Jesus knew that God had given all things into His hands. We can have that assurance, too. All that we need or could ever desire, God has promised us. He sent His Son to die for us and to give us eternal life. Salvation is ours. He gives us His grace. His joy. His peace. His hope. The desires of our hearts (see Psalm 37:4). He promises to take care of our daily necessities, such as food and clothing, telling us not to worry about what we eat or wear because He knows our needs. He has promised us strength to do all things.

Second, Jesus knew that He had come from God. That He

belonged to God. That God was His Father. He taught His disciples to address God as *Abba*, "Father." He called us His children, His sons and daughters. We came from God. He loves us exactly the way we are—with the freckles, talents, and personalities that we have.

Third, Jesus knew He was going to the Father. He knew that this life wasn't permanent. That He was just passing through. That His mission here was to do God's will. Real life is in heaven with His Father. It doesn't matter what people think or do to us here. What matters is that we're headed home. God even tells us to encourage one another with the fact that He is coming for us (1 Thessalonians 4:18). Not only are we going to the Father, He has prepared the way for us and will make us ready (see Philippians 1:6). And He will come and get us. This world is not our home. We're just camping out. Soon we're headed home. If we focus on the fact that we're going to be with our Father soon, then we can put this life into proper perspective. If we look at our schedules in the light of eternal life, it will be easier to keep things where they belong.

Knowing Who we belong to, what He's done for us, and where we're going gives our lives focus. Having the latest fashion here doesn't mean as much as the robe we'll wear there. A huge house on this earth loses its luster in comparison with the mansion God is building for us in heaven. I'm finding that as I focus on the real purpose of this life—preparing for the next world and sharing that glorious opportunity with others—a lot of things here lose their importance. What becomes most important to me is spending time with people.

My kids. My family. My friends. Ministering the way God has called me to minister. Investing in people's lives. Making a difference. Not attempting to acquire material things.

6. *Be accountable.* "Accountability" isn't a very popular word today. We like to do our own thing and answer to no one. But accountability helps us to grow and meet the goals we believe God wants us to achieve. But how do we become accountable?

For me, I need people to help me be accountable. Trusted people that I know love me. So I depend on a couple of close friends. Many times, I ask them to hold me accountable to something specific. When I was attempting to cut back demands on my time that weren't part of what God had called me to do, I shared with my friend Tanya a specific job that I needed to quit. I hate letting someone down, and I wanted to finish the project. So after much struggle and prayer, I decided that I wouldn't take on any new projects once this one was finished. I asked Tanya to keep me accountable for this decision. She could ask me if I quit. If I didn't, she could remind me that I had said I was going to quit. Having Tanya to help me be accountable enabled me to follow through on my decision.

Sue is my prayer partner; we've been praying together for years. She knows me better than almost anyone else. She knows my strengths and weaknesses and loves me despite them all. Sue is a constant source of encouragement and a source of accountability. As we talk together, she will often ask me, "Is this something God wants you to do?" She knows that I like to be involved and busy, but that more than anything else, I want to spend my time the way God wants me to. So she asks.

Tina is another friend who holds me accountable. She helps me watch my time and assess new projects. She holds me accountable for the details of what I need to be doing—reminding me, encouraging me. She also holds me accountable for being honest. Just today, I got a note from her because she cared. She thought I looked tired and discouraged at church and just wanted to remind me that she cares. She asked me how my personal relationship with God was coming along. She makes sure that I'm taking the time I need to keep that connection strong. She asks because she cares.

Who can hold you accountable? Find someone you trust—a close friend, a spouse, a prayer partner. It's important that it be someone you know loves you so that when they ask you the tough questions, you won't be offended or hurt. You'll know that they've asked because they care.

How does someone hold you accountable? By asking questions about the things for which you have specifically asked to be held accountable and for things they know are important to you. By praying for you and with you. By reminding you of what's important to you. By keeping those commitments before you constantly. When we know someone is going to be asking us about a thing, it motivates us to do something about it. Last year, my mom lost fifty pounds through Weight Watchers. She had attempted earlier to do it on her own. She knew the program from doing it before. But she said, "I can't do it without the meetings. Without having to weigh in." Knowing that someone else was keeping track of how she was doing kept her committed to her goal.

It's the same with each of us. Being accountable to someone

keeps us committed to the goal.

When our lives are out of balance and we just can't keep everything balanced any longer, where do we begin?

By being real. By being the person God made us to be.

By being radical. By not conforming to the world but by living up to God's standards.

By being simple. By living a simpler life. Less demands. Fewer bills. Living within our means—financially and time wise.

By being firm. By saying No and sticking to our priorities.

By being focused. Focused on what God wants. On our ultimate goal—eternal life—not a big house or a huge bank account.

By being accountable. By having a trusted friend walk beside us and help us on our journey.

Thinking and Talking About It

1. How balanced is your life? Is it out of balance?

2. What is your purpose? Who has God created you to be? What gifts and talents has He given you? What are the most important things in your life?

3. Why are you doing what you're doing? What are your motives? Is this what God wants? What are your priorities? Your goals?

4. Whose expectations does your life meet—the world's or God's? What are the most important things God wants you to accomplish?

5. How could you simplify your life? Are you living within your means? How much time do you spend at home?

6. How do you decide what to say Yes to or No to? Do your decisions reflect trust in God?

7. Do you base your decisions on the ultimate goal—eternal life? How would doing so change your decisions?

8. Do you have someone to be accountable to? If not, who could you be accountable to?

CHAPTER FOUR

The Number One Priority

For me, spending time with God is my number one priority. At least that's what I say. Too often, my schedule hasn't reflected that priority. Other, more "urgent" things have bumped my time with God from my schedule. Or I've filled my days so full that I stay up late and can't get up early. Whatever the cause, time with God has been something I long for but that has been hard to find.

As I began working on finding balance in my life, I thought the answer would be simple. All I had to do was to make my time with Him a priority. Schedule it. Get up for it. And if I didn't manage to spend time with Him in the early morning hours, at least I would do so before I did anything else—after doing what absolutely couldn't wait, of course. All it would take to find spiritual balance in my life was to make sure I spent that time with God, right?

I soon realized that it is so much more than that. It's not only making time a priority, but there must be a balance in how I view that time. I had an extensive quiet time with God using all kinds of disciplines. At that point in my life, I felt that a good quiet time meant including many steps. First, praising God through my praise journal. I used a student's daily planner with spaces for each day of the week. Each morning, I began my quiet time by filling those spaces with things from the day before—big or little—for which I could thank God. I always made sure that I filled the entire space. That was my goal.

Second, I read the current day's reading from the women's devotional. Later, I added a devotional from the Christian classic, *My Utmost for His Highest*. It seemed others were getting so much from this little book that I thought I'd be a better Christian if I read it too.

Third, I journaled. Using a spiral bound notebook, I wrote out a prayer to God in letter form, pouring out my heart, all my thoughts and feelings, struggles, desires, and hopes. After that came my prayer notebook. This is where I kept all my prayer requests—my prayer list—divided into the days of the week. I prayed for a portion of the list each day; it was long, so it took awhile, even praying for just part of the list. By the time I finished all of this, it was time for Bible study. Many days I would want to quit when I got to this point. All the disciplines took so long, and my to do list for the day was looming before me. Often, too, I didn't know what to study or where to begin. So sometimes I quit. Sometimes I skimmed through my study just to be able to say I had done it, but it wasn't meaningful.

Although all the disciplines were good and often brought me closer to God, my quiet time had become a to do list in itself—something I could check off as I did each part. And if I didn't check everything off, then I felt I hadn't done it right. Time with God became a chore, not a relationship.

Over a period of months, as I struggled with feelings of being overwhelmed, of having too much to do and not enough time, the disciplines became a requirement I just couldn't meet. I didn't have the energy for it all. I dreaded my quiet time and the time it would take. I just couldn't do it all, and I felt guilty because I thought I should.

During this time, however, my relationship with God grew stronger. I knew beyond the shadow of a doubt that He was still there. I could feel His presence and see Him at work. Meanwhile, my quiet time was changing. There were mornings when I didn't open a book or a journal. I just listened to music. One CD in particular came to mean so much to me. The music touched chords in my heart, causing me to pray, worship, and think. It challenged me with ideas. All I had to do was turn on the music and listen— and I could feel my heart being drawn to God as I worshiped Him.

When I did sit down to have a regular quiet time, I let go of the disciplines. I just couldn't face them all. I cut back to the basics, the things that were most important to me. I continued to keep the praise journal, but filling the space was no longer my focus. I focused on praising God. The funny thing was, as I let go of the requirement and let my thoughts focus on God alone, the spaces in my praise journal became full and often overflowing. I continued journaling. For me, journaling is like breathing. It's the easiest way for me to communicate. Writing keeps me focused so my mind doesn't wander. It helps me expand on what I'm thinking and feeling and determine the real issues in my heart.

There were times when I prayed aloud. Once, I pulled up the empty rocking chair and invited God to join me, talking to Him aloud as if He was right there. (And He was—I just couldn't see Him.) Then I studied my Bible. God's Word is so important to me. I want to be in it. I want it in me.

About this time, I was preparing a camp meeting seminar on how to get into God's Word. As I studied the Bible for myself, I looked for what made it meaningful to me. I tried new ways of studying. And God blessed. One week, I paraphrased Psalms. I planned to present paraphrasing as one of the methods in my seminar, but I actually thought it would be difficult and the method I would dislike most. But as I paraphrased God's Word on my own during my quiet time, the verses caused me to worship God, to praise Him and focus on Him. And that is what Bible study is all about—learning to know God more, to focus on Him. It's a book about God, not just a bunch of stories. It tells us not so much how to live as Who to live for. It's not about the characters and how they triumphed with God's help. It's about a God who worked in ordinary people's lives and caused extraordinary things to happen. It's about Him. And Bible study needs to help us to know Him more.

One day I did a topical study of the word *satisfy*. I wanted God to satisfy the needs of my heart. That's when I found a verse that challenged me right where I was. As I paraphrased it, I wrote, "Why do you run to bread to satisfy you? Why do you waste your money on things that can never satisfy you? God alone can." In my emptiness, too often I turned to food, especially chocolate, to satisfy my need. What I truly needed was God. And as I let go of all my self-made requirements and sought Him from the emptiness of my soul, I found Him in huge, satisfying ways.

I learned to turn my thoughts more and more toward God during the day. It was almost like having a running conversation with Him throughout the day. I had often prayed, "God go with me throughout my day" as I ended my quiet time. But I realized that I didn't really need to ask Him to go with me. *He* was *always* with me. *I* needed to stay with Him. Not run ahead. Not get so busy that I forgot all about Him until I met with Him the next morning or mumbled a few words to Him out of habit as I fell asleep at night.

Finding balance in my quiet time has meant more than just making my time with God a priority. That is part of it, of course, and we need to have that time and to be committed to it. But finding balance in my devotional life means realizing that what I must have with God is a relationship, not a list of requirements. God never made a list of things I needed to do each morning or evening in order to have a "good" quiet time with Him. Even though all the disciplines I included in my devotional time were good, they couldn't take the place of a relationship. If I became caught up in having to do all the right things, I couldn't truly think about or seek a relationship with God. I had been trying to live up to a standard, and that is not what it is all about. It's about a relationship.

God wants a relationship with us. A friendship. A parent-child relationship. A marriage. These are all ways He has used to describe our relationship with Him. He wants us to see Him as a Friend, a Father, a Husband. A Being who is intimately involved in our lives. One who cares about every detail that matters to us. He wants us to share our thoughts, our feelings, our hopes, and our dreams. And He wants us to enter into this kind of a relationship because we want to—not because we have to. Because we love Him, and because He loves us. He doesn't require us to accomplish a certain list of things. He just wants us to come to Him. To seek Him. He says, "search for Me with all your heart. I will be found by you" (Jeremiah 29:13, 14, NKJV). He doesn't even require us to put in a certain number of hours of service. He just wants us. He'll take care of the rest.

Not only can our devotional time become a list of requirements to check off instead of a relationship—so can our service and our worship. Stacy Rinehart writes, "The average person feels this heavy weight of excessive expectation. If he's not careful, his life will become a revolving door of Bible studies, personal evangelism programs, committee meetings, seminars, and financial pleas. He must have a regular quiet time, pray for many hours, get involved in missions, be a great parent, disciple new believers, and more. The weight of these 'ought-to's' becomes almost more than he can bear. Many people have tried with good hearts and sincere intentions to comply, without success. Some have even left the church, feeling inadequate and thoroughly unspiritual" (*Upside Down: The Paradox of Servant Leadership*, pp. 117, 118).

How many times have we let others (and ourselves) pile up the expectations that form our idea of what it means to be a good Christian? How often do our lists crush us and others as we attempt to live up to standards and requirements that God has never put on us? Get up early. Have a long devotional time, reading the Bible and praying for others. Eat a certain way. Never lose our tempers.

Never say a mean word—not even about the driver who cuts us off. And on and on we go with details huge and small, expecting perfection. Making a list and checking it twice. Forgetting that only God can make us perfect. That He changes us slowly. "Too slowly," we think, as we try to help the process along, attempting to live the way we think we should.

Most of the time, of course, there is nothing wrong with our expectations. We *should* study and pray. We *do* need to learn to control our tempers and our words. We *do* want to be good parents and disciple new believers. But when the requirements become more important than the relationship, then we have lost balance. When we're so focused on living a certain way that we forget the One whom we are supposed to be getting to know, then we have lost balance.

God wants a relationship with you and me just the way we are. Right now. Not after we've got it all together. Not only if we meet all the requirements. He's promised to complete the work in us. To supply all our needs—including the need to grow and change. He's promised to give us the strength to do all that He asks of us. Our part is to allow Him to do the work.

We need to come to the place that we can let go of other people's expectations of us—and even more importantly, of what we *think* they expect of us, which is often more than they really expect. We need to let go of our own expectations, which are usually more demanding than those of anyone else. Then we need to just look to God and ask, "What does *He* expect?"

God expects us to fail. He expects us to fall down. He knew all along that we would. That is why He sent a Savior while we were still sinners. And God views us differently than we see ourselves. He sees our hearts. He knows what we long to be and do. He knows how very much we want to know Him. Maybe He's saying, "Let go of what you think you have to do, and just be with Me."

That is what I've been trying to do—let go of all the requirements and focus on the relationship. I'm realizing that my quiet time can vary from day to day in content and that each day I can learn about God in a new way. Whether it's my traditional meet-You-in-the-morning-with-my-worship-basket or praising God through music or just walking in the woods or sitting on the back step watching the kittens play and praising Him for all He's done and created— these are all ways of spending time with Him. That is what He desires—for me to spend time with Him. To focus my thoughts on Him. To share all that is in my heart. To listen for His voice. There is no one right way to do it. I just need to do it.

And as I serve Him, I need to follow the same principle. I don't serve because it's expected or because it's required, but because I love Him. He has planned that I will serve Him in a way that is unique to me. He created me differently than anyone else so that I would fit the particular part of His puzzle that He designed for me. I may be doing a job that someone else is doing or has done, but I will always do it with my particular flair. There are no cookie-cutter ministries with God. He gives each of us a passion and gifts and talents, which when combined allow us to find our unique place. I'm learning that although I have the gift of organization and administration, my passion is people. So I don't enjoy using my gifts in serving on committees as much as I enjoy using them in events that minister to people. It isn't planning an event that makes me excited, it's the possibility of God affecting people through the event that is exciting.

We need to find balance in our lives, not only so that we can have a relationship with God but in order to make sure that it is a relationship and not simply something we do as a requirement. God doesn't want our quiet time with Him or our service for Him to be just another item to check off our list of things to do. He wants us to take time to grow closer to Him. Whether it's sitting at His feet, walking with Him, or serving Him, each is an opportunity to know Him better. True balance comes in taking the time to build our friendship with Him instead of seeing time with Him as just another thing to check off our list.

Thinking and Talking About It

1. If you were to describe the perfect Christian, how would you picture her? How do you think God would describe the perfect Christian? Compare the two descriptions.

2. What are your expectations for your quiet time with God? Do you sometimes let these expectations become more important than the relationship itself?

3. Describe an occasion when you spent time with God in a meaningful way.

4. List the ways you serve God. Why do you serve Him in this way? Are these the areas where your gifts or talents lie? Are you doing these things because you feel that you are expected to? Because no one else will? Because it is a job that has to be done?

5. Look back over your list. Are there things there that God hasn't called you to do? Is it possible to let go of those activities?

CHAPTER FIVE

Where Do I Go to Resign?

To Whom It May Concern:

I hereby officially tender my resignation as an adult. I have decided I would like to accept the responsibilities of a six-year-old again.

I want to go to McDonald's and think that it's a four star restaurant.

I want to sail sticks across a fresh mud puddle and make ripples with rocks.

I want to think M&Ms are better than money because you can eat them.

I want to play kickball during recess and paint with watercolors in art.

I want to lie under a big oak tree and run a lemonade stand with my friends on a hot summer day.

I want to return to a time when life was simple. When all you knew were colors, addition tables, and simple nursery rhymes—but that didn't *bother you, because you didn't know what you didn't know, and you didn't care. When all you knew was to be happy because you didn't know all the things that should make you worried and upset.*

I want to think that the world is fair—that everyone in it is honest and good. I want to believe that anything is possible.

Somewhere in my youth I matured, and I learned too much.

I learned of nuclear weapons, war, prejudice, starvation, and abused children.

I learned of lies, unhappy marriages, suffering, illness, pain, and death.

I learned of a world in which children knew how to kill—and did.

What happened to the time when we thought that everyone would live forever because we didn't grasp the concept of death? When we thought that the worst thing in the world was for someone to take the jump rope from us or to pick us last for kickball?

I want to be oblivious to the complexity of life and be overly excited by little things once again. I want to return to the days when reading was fun and music was clean. When television was used to report the news or for family entertainment and not to promote sex, violence, and deceit.

I remember being naive and thinking that everyone was happy because I was. I didn't worry about time, bills, or where I was going to find the money to fix my car. I used to wonder what I was going to do or be when I grew up—not worry about what I'll do if this doesn't work out.

I want to live simply again. I don't want my day to consist of computer crashes, mountains of paperwork, depressing news, how to survive more

days in the month than there is money in the bank, doctor bills, gossip,
illness, and loss of loved ones. I want to believe in the power of smiles,
hugs, a kind word, truth, justice, peace, dreams, the imagination,
mankind, and making angels in the snow.

I want to be six again.—Author unknown.

Someone sent the above thoughts to me via e-mail. It was titled
"Where Do I Go to Resign?" Sometimes I've asked myself the same
question—and many of the questions in the piece. There are days
when I just want to quit—quit being a grown-up, quit being involved
in whatever I'm involved in. My friends know that when I'm stressed
out and ready to give up, I say, "I'm going to quit and go work at
Taco Bell." (I choose Taco Bell because that is where Zack wanted
me to work when he was six. He loved the food and wanted me to
bring some home every night.) In my mind, working at Taco Bell
would mean going to a job in which I could put in my hours and
come home, leaving work behind. No one calling me late at night.
No letters complaining about how I did something. No one wanting
me to do more. No one would know where I lived to ask me to turn
the seven-layer burrito into an eight-layer one!

Sometimes quitting sounds like the answer. As we melt into a
heap of exhaustion at the end of the day, we just want to quit—
something, anything, everything. We just don't want to be
responsible any more.

But we don't quit. We keep trudging along, attempting to carry
all that we've been asked to do. And also trying to accomplish all
that we haven't been asked to do, but think we need to do. We take

on more and more without letting go of anything, until we're juggling so many things that we begin to drop them.

How do we know when to quit? And what to quit?

These are questions I've asked myself many times. I love most of what I'm doing. And I hate quitting something. If I quit, who is going to take it over? What if no one wants to do it? What if it doesn't get done? What if I quit the wrong things?

But when life is overwhelming and out of balance, something has to give. How do we know what to do?

1. Pray. The first thing I do is pray. I want to make sure that I'm doing the thing God wants me to do. He has promised to give me wisdom. "If any of you lacks wisdom, let him ask of God, who gives to all liberally and without reproach, and it will be given to him" (James 1:5, NKJV). God promises to give us wisdom liberally. He isn't stingy. He doesn't want to keep us guessing or wondering. He wants us to make our decisions wisely.

God cares about our schedules. He knows that there is wisdom in being careful with how we schedule our days. The psalmist prayed, "So teach *us* to number our days, That we may gain a heart of wisdom" (Psalm 90:12, NKJV, emphasis added). There is wisdom in numbering our days. There is wisdom in knowing that our time on this earth is short and that we need to make the best of it. Live life wisely, not futilely—not spending time running and being busy without making a difference but in doing what God has planned for you to do.

Each morning I pray and give God my plans for that day. I list all that I want to accomplish and give it to Him. I ask Him to give me *His* plans for my day. Then I go through my day, trusting Him with it. I trust that the interruptions are His interruptions. I accept that the delays and problems are all a part of what He desires for me. At the end of the day, if I haven't finished all I wanted to do, I let it go, believing that God has planned my day His way.

That is what we can do with our list of responsibilities—lay them all out before God and say, "Here they are, Lord, all the things I want to do and need to do. Show me what You want." The psalmist prayed a similar prayer, "And let the beauty of the Lord our God be upon us, And establish the work of our hands for us; Yes, establish the work of our hands" (Psalm 90:17, NKJV). Trust God to establish the work you should do. That leads to the next step.

2. Decide if it is a part of God's plan. Do the things I'm attempting to accomplish fit with what God wants me to do? How do I know what God wants me to do?

I know that what God desires will always fit with His Word; He will never ask me to do anything contrary to the Scriptures. I also know that He has promised to give me the gifts and talents to accomplish what He plans for me to do. And I know that He does have plans for me. The Bible tells me so. But what are His plans?

I know that foremost in God's plan is for me to have a relationship with Him through His Word and His Son. There is no denying it. He longs to have a relationship with me. With you. That is more important to Him than any other thing. So important that He sent His Son to die for it. Then sent His Spirit to help us grow and learn. He even sends His angels to minister to us (see Hebrews 1:14). I know that if God were to plan my day, it would always include time with Him.

As a wife and a mother, I know that God wants me to take care of my home and family. There are many Scripture texts that talk about our roles as wives and mothers. These roles are so important to Him that He commands the older women to teach the younger ones how to love their husbands and children and how to be good homemakers (see Titus 2:3-5). I believe our families are our first mission field. I believe that if God were to plan my day, He would plan for me to take the time not only to care for my family's physical needs but to talk with them and play with them and hug them.

So there are these two roles to which I'm certain God has called me. After that, things get a little fuzzy. But His Word still has guidelines for me.

He tells us that He has given us gifts and talents that we are to use in building up His church. And He has commanded us to go and tell the world about Him, teaching them how to do what He has commanded (see Matthew 28:19, 20). How do I figure out how this fits in my life?

Jesus said that He came to give us life more abundantly and to make our joy full. So I don't think God would call us to do anything we would hate or think of as drudgery. I believe that what He calls us to do will be something that we will enjoy. I read recently that when we're doing what God has called us to do, we will feel that we're doing what we were created to do. And we will be.

I've known since I was a little girl that I wanted to write. I wrote all the time, even writing stories for my friends' writing assignments. As I grew, I used my love for writing to write notes to others. But the desire to write continued to grow until I finally attempted to write a book. It was hard work, and the first manuscript was rewritten three times before it was published. After I began writing, others affirmed that God was using this ability to touch their lives as they shared with me how something they read had special meaning to them or changed them somehow. So I had the desire, the ability, and affirmation from others.

I've also always loved to sing. I sing a lot—in the shower, in the car, around the house. I have the desire; I would love to be able to sing for special music. But I don't have the ability to sing by myself in front of people. I can carry a tune, but vocal music is not my gift or talent. And although my son, Zack, thinks I sing wonderfully, there hasn't been much affirmation for my singing talent. Thus regretfully, I've realized that although I can praise God with my singing, it's not a ministry He has called me to carry out for Him.

Sometimes God calls us to something that we don't have a desire to do—at least not at first. I never planned on public speaking. If you had known me in high school, you would understand. I was so shy! I hated getting up in front. My knees knocked, and my stomach quaked. If anyone had told me, then, what I would be doing now, I wouldn't have believed them. My mother says she wouldn't have believed it either. So when God opened up opportunities for me to speak, I felt sick to my stomach. As I drove to my first speaking appointment at a church in my community, I kept asking myself, "Why am I doing this?" But once I started, it felt natural. I enjoyed it. Afterwards, all the way home I kept asking myself, "Why did I do that? I'll never do it again!" But I knew I would. I knew that even though I had never thought I would want to speak or enjoy speaking, I did. And the affirmation again came.

When God calls us to do something, He will give us the ability, the peace (or desire,) and, often, affirmation from others.

Sometimes we think that because we are capable of doing something that means we need to do it. We believe if God gave us the talent to do a thing, then we have to do it. But that is not necessarily true. We may be capable of doing a lot of things, but God has not necessarily called us to all of them. My friend, Tina, has many talents and abilities. She has a drive to get things done and does them well and with enthusiasm. I believe that she could take any position in the church and do a great job at it. But that doesn't mean that God has called her to fill all the positions in the church. Besides giving us talents and gifts, God gives us passion—a caring about something. Tina cares about people, especially the women in our church—those who are no longer attending and those who are attending but who aren't involved. Combining her gifts and passion, Tina is right at home in Women's Ministries.

Janet's passion is prayer. God has mightily used her passion for prayer, combined with her leadership and wisdom skills, in prayer conferences and retreats. Sue has a special place in her heart for those who are hurting. She has the gift of encouragement and teaching. She has found her niche working for a crisis phone line. Not only does she answer phones, but she trains others to listen and respond. Tanya is creative, and she has a heart for children. I think that is why she has been asked to help lead Vacation Bible School and Cradle Roll in the last two churches she has attended.

God calls us to serve Him by using our talents and gifts in ways that are exciting to us and in areas that we care about. And He will often affirm our call by the words of others and by showing us how our ministry has touched the lives of others.

How does knowing this help us to know what to quit and what to do?

Make a list of all the roles and responsibilities you currently hold. Pray about them. Give them to God. Then look at each one in the light of your gifts and passion. Decide, "Has God called me to this, giving me a desire to do it, an excitement or passion for it? Do I have the gifts and the talents? Do I have the time to give it all the responsibility it requires?"

As I looked over my own list of responsibilities recently, I found several things that I needed to let go. One was something I was very capable of doing, but I didn't enjoy it. It was work, and it took up time from things I knew God *had* called me to. So I quit. Two other things I felt I should let go were positions at church that I had enjoyed doing at one time. And at one time, I knew God had called me to do them. But I was no longer effective. I didn't have the needed time or energy to give to these demands. I needed to step down either from these positions or from something else in my schedule. But there was nothing else on my list that I felt I could let go. So I quit these two positions. When I told my friend, Cecelia, what I had done, she said, "Good for you. I'm proud of you!" I appreciated the affirmation. Quitting was hard for me. I didn't want to let anyone down or disappoint them. But I was letting people down by holding positions that I just couldn't do well. And I was letting myself down by being stressed about things I could no longer handle.

I believe that when God calls us to do something, He will give us the desire or a sense of peace about it. He has also promised to give us the gifts and talents. Many times we may not feel that we have the ability, but God has promised. He may call us to do something we feel totally incapable of doing. But if He calls us, He will equip us. The ability may not come first. We may not realize that we are capable until we have stepped out in faith and obedience to accept His call. But always, God will make us able. There will be joy and excitement in serving God the way He desires. We will get excited talking about it. It will be fun—not all the time, of course. There will be times when the frustrations and discouragements loom large. But we will know deep down inside that it is what we love doing. Often, God will affirm what we are doing. But watch out. There will also be times when people will tell us we are doing a great job, and we are not where God wants us to be. Remember, we are often capable of doing things God has not called us to do. Affirmation is an added bonus—not the defining sign.

3. *If it is not part of His plan, quit.* If God hasn't called you to do a thing, don't. As you look over your list, if God nudges your heart to stop something, then stop it. It may be hard to quit. Like me, you might not want to disappoint people. Remind yourself that you are disappointing God by continuing to do something He hasn't asked you to do. Remind yourself that He may have someone else He wants to do it, and you are in the way. But what if there isn't anyone else to do it? How can you quit if no one else is willing to do it? It's a matter of trust. How much do you trust God? Do you trust Him enough to believe that He will always accomplish what He

wants done through the means He chooses? If He wants something to happen, He will provide the people and resources. And if He doesn't, then it's not something He wanted. We need to let go and trust Him.

There will be times when it's time to quit something that God has called us to. But our part is over, and it's time to move on. We have done what He wanted, and now it's time for us to do something else. That is OK. It's like being a parent. God blesses us with a child to raise. A child to love and care for, to encourage and teach and discipline. But inevitably, there comes a day when that child will move out of our home. A phase in our parenting is over. While we will always be their parent—and they will always be our child—we have to let go and stop parenting the way we did when they were little. There may be times God will call us to do something for a time and then call us to do something different. When that happens, it's time to follow His leading.

4. Don't take on anything new without letting go of something else. If we continually take on new responsibilities without letting something else go, our lives will become out of balance. If both sides of a scale weigh the same, the scale is balanced. But add something to one side, without taking something off the other, and the scale is tipped. That is how our lives can become as well. We keep adding more and more things to do; more and more expectations of ourselves. Don't take on anything new—big or small—without praying about it and considering if it is what God wants you to do. Many times it's the small things that throw us off. A little thing here and a little thing there, and pretty soon our schedules are too full. If, after prayer, the new role or appointment is something you believe that God wants you to take, then let something else go. Prayerfully consider what can wait, be put off, or ended.

5. Don't take on anything you don't have time to pray about. Never accept a new responsibility without praying about it—even if it's only a quick prayer about an invitation for lunch with a friend. Make it a habit to pray about your schedule and responsibilities. Keep a list of your roles and jobs handy to pray about on a regular basis. Constantly taking all you do before God will often help you to see more clearly what is most important.

After you have prayed about it, don't stop praying even if God leads you to take it on. Continue to pray. Pray for wisdom as you proceed. Pray for those involved with you. Pray for the plans and ideas you will need. Part of my weekly prayer list includes each of the different ministries and projects in which I'm involved. I pray for my Sabbath School class and for each of the kids by name. I pray for those helping me. I pray for discipline and for the curriculum. I pray that the students will learn how to have a real and vital relationship with God. I pray for the Women's Ministries leaders I work with. I pray for the conference leaders in our union, for the leaders at the division level, for the local leaders within my conference. I pray that God will give me plans and ideas; that He will show me how to lead and what to plan. I pray for my current writing projects and for future writing projects I have planned. I pray for the books I've already written and the people who will read them. If you don't have time to pray for the projects you're involved in, whether it's ministry, home, or work, then you're too involved. We can't do anything the way God wants us to unless we regularly go to Him for guidance. We can't just ask Him once and then head out on our own. We need His constant direction.

6. The "have-to's." Our days will always have things we have to do—jobs, housework, answering the phone. They may not seem like part of God's plan for us, but they have to be done. But as we give our days to Him, many of the "have-to's" can become part of His plan. Our work may become a place to use our gift for prayer by praying for our co-workers or customers. The housework becomes an act of worship as we do it for Him, dedicating our home to Him. And even the telemarketers on the phone can be part of His plan as we become one of the few nice people they talk to in the day.

Some things have to get done. But they don't have to be top priority. They don't have to require all our energy and focus. As we pray for God's will to be done in our lives and as we put things in proper perspective, we will learn to do what we have to do but also to make time for the truly important—whatever that may be for each of us.

Where do we go to resign?

We go to God in prayer, asking for wisdom and seeking to know what He has called us to do—and letting go of the rest.

Thinking and Talking About It

1. Have you ever felt like quitting or resigning?

2. Make a list of all your roles and responsibilities. (You may still have the list you made in one of the previous chapters.) Then make

a list of the gifts and talents God has given you. Think about what you most care about—your passion.

3. Now take both your list of roles and the list of your talents and passions, and compare them prayerfully, asking God for wisdom. How does what you're actually doing harmonize with your gifts and the things you are passionate about? Have people affirmed you in these areas?

4. Have you taken on new responsibilities without letting go of old ones? Do you have time to pray about all you are doing?

5. Look at the roles and responsibilities that you aren't able to do as effectively as you would like. Are these roles that God may be leading you to quit doing? What would it take to let them go? Can you do that?

CHAPTER SIX

Finding Time for Family and Friends

Often, when our lives are out of balance with myriad things to do and demands to meet and places to be, family and friends get pushed aside. We don't mean to do that. We don't want to. And often, we don't even realize that we are neglecting the people most important to us. But as we have more and more to do, we have less and less time for people.

One of the hazards of an out-of-balance life is overwork. A forty-hour work week may be normal, but many of us are working more than forty hours. My brother has been putting in sixty hours a week lately. His business has picked up, and there is more work to do than employees to do it. Another brother works two jobs. Of course, we have to work to provide for our families. But although all the extra hours may mean that we are contributing bigger paychecks to our families, we may not be giving them what they really need—time with us.

I've read that children spell love, T-I-M-E. They want time with us—not quality time, but quantity time. They want to do things with us, not have more toys to play with. A couple of summers ago, we took the boys on vacation. Unfortunately, this isn't something we've done often. We headed for the Great Smoky Mountains, a place Tim and I had been to several times. We hiked. We went to Cherokee, North Carolina and saw the incredible outdoor play, "Unto These Hills." The boys loved it. When we got home, I asked them, "What was the most fun thing you did on vacation?" They both had the same answer: "The water slide with Dad!" At the campground, where we pitched our tent, was a water slide. One afternoon, we decided to give it a try. The boys had a blast. The thing that was ironic to me was that there is a water slide fifteen minutes from our house. We drove twelve hours and did all kinds of things on our vacation. Yet what they enjoyed most could have been done at home. It wasn't the fact that we went on vacation or that we went some place new and exciting. What they enjoyed most was playing with Dad on the water slide.

Our busyness affects the amount of time we spend with our children. Sometimes I think we would be surprised at how much time we actually spend together with them—especially fathers. I'm not talking about the time we spend telling them to do their homework, pick up their rooms, or brush their teeth. How much time do we spend playing with them? Reading a book to them or with them. How much time do we spend talking with them—not at them—about the things that are important to them. One of the things I love about the end of the day is spending a few minutes with the boys in their room. As I tuck them in, I ask what I can pray about for them. I ask them about their day and linger a few minutes to listen. It's amazing how our children will open up and talk to us when given the opportunity, when they know that we're really listening. During the school year, I drive the boys back and forth to school. I'd love to be able to put them on the bus, but because they go to a private school that is twelve miles from our public school line, we don't receive bussing. Yet even though having to make that trip is tiring and an interruption in my day, I cherish those moments. The boys and I have talked about so many important things in the car. Some of our best conversations have taken place on the way to or from school. It's a time when they have my attention. I'm not going anywhere, and neither are they.

And it isn't just our kids who want time with us. Our spouses do, too. I love to spend time with Tim. To have his attention. To have him really listen and hear what I'm saying. To have him talk with me. I like doing things with him—fun things, not just working around the house. I like going out for dinner—just the two of us. Or walking around our country block, holding hands and talking.

And of course, there are friends and other family members—parents, aunts, uncles, siblings, grandparents. How do we fit everyone in?

1.Realize how important time with people is. Without time together, we won't know our children or be there for them when they have to make difficult decisions. They won't come to us for advice. They will get their information from their peers—often a scary thought, especially when they are teenagers. That is the time we often begin to give them more freedom, which is important, but it is also a time for parents to remain involved and informed. Without spending time with our kids, we will miss out on so much. They grow so quickly. My boys have brought me so much joy and laughter. I don't want to miss a moment of it.

Without time together with our spouses, they will feel neglected. Our marriages won't be strong. We may drift so far apart that we won't really know each other any more and may not care if we spend time together or not. We need time to focus on each other. To show love. To feel loved. To know why we're doing all of this in the first place.

We need our friends and other family members more than we realize. Friends help keep us sane and give us someone to talk to, lean on, and play with. Christian friends also give us someone to pray with and someone to pray for us in times of crisis. Last week, my brother was in an accident that severed a finger and parts of three others. It was traumatic. I knew immediately that I could call friends and there would be people praying for him. Tina prayed with me on the phone, holding up my brother, his wife and daughters, and me before God. At church, the people in our prayer chain asked Tim and me how my brother was doing. It reminded me that people care. That is something important for each of us to remember. We're not in this alone. Friends help carry us through, and they need our help to carry them. God has told us to bear one another's burdens, to encourage one another and build each other up. Friends are a part of God's plan for us.

2. Realize the hazards of not spending time with people. When I'm really busy, it affects the whole family. The kids are left to play on their own. It's true that they need to be able to play on their own without constant entertainment by me, but they also need me to be involved in their lives. They love playing games with me or even helping me in the kitchen—getting the opportunity to talk to me. When they are left to play on their own for too long, trouble erupts. They begin picking on each other. Fighting. Getting carried away and doing things they shouldn't. They can get so silly with each other. Inevitably, something or someone gets hurt.

When I'm too busy, I tend to get short-tempered. I yell at the kids or lose my patience. I forget that the children are my priority and see them, instead, as an interruption to an over-full day. That's not what I want. I want to enjoy my kids. I want them to know that they are more important to me than anything else. I want them to know that if they need me, they can interrupt me—without me yelling at them or acting frustrated. They know that I have things to do. They've learned to respect the time Mom or Dad needs to put into a project or work. But they need to have the assurance that although we may need to finish something we are doing, ultimately, they are more important than any project.

In our marriage, both Tim and I feel neglected when the other is too busy. We lose the intimacy that makes a marriage strong. Without spending time together, reconnecting with each other on a regular basis, we find our marriage coasts downhill, turning lovers into strangers, making it difficult to face the trials and problems we must deal with as couples. Instead of feeling like a team, we feel hurt, frustrated, and alone.

Aloneness also results from not having time for friends. When we don't invest time in them, our friendships lose their closeness. Eventually, we may not have friends at all. Then when we face a crisis or a lonely moment—or have a joy to share—there is no one there. Neither is there anyone to share his or her joys or struggles with us. Our life becomes nothing more than attempting to accomplish things. There is no one with whom to share those accomplishments.

3. Set boundaries. Finding time for family and friends won't happen by itself. We never just find time, and if we could, it would be only little snatches here and there. People are too important to give them the leftovers from a too-busy schedule. People make life important—not the things we are involved with. So instead of finding time for people, we have to make it. Schedule it in. Put it on our calendars. And then let nothing interrupt it. We need time at home together as a family with nothing planned. We need time when each of us can do the things we have to do at home while interacting with each other. Bumping into each other.

We have a couple of house rules to protect our family time. One regards the phone. We don't answer the phone during dinner, family worship, or "date" times for Tim and me. Dinner is a time for our family to sit down together at the end of the day and catch up. We've had to change the hour we eat a couple of times in order to mesh with Tim's work schedule. But unless he's working really late, we wait for him. The phone rings often during dinner. Usually it's a salesperson, but not always. We let the answering machine pick up. Later, we return the call if necessary. Our friends know that if they call in the evening and we don't answer, we're probably eating dinner. At least one other family has adopted this rule for themselves.

It's the same with family worship and our "date" times—we just don't answer the phone. We let the answering machine pick it up. It's our way of saying that nothing is more important than our time together. Admittedly, we occasionally pick up the phone if we're expecting an important call. When the boys were away at camp, they usually called during meal times, and I picked up the phone every time it rang. I didn't want to miss their calls.

Friday night is our family night. We have a special dinner with dessert. We've used candles and goblets and, at times, even have included Sabbath blessings from a book of Jewish traditions. After dinner, we play games together or go for a walk or read a book. There are lots of great books out there for kids. We choose Christian historical fiction series written for early teens. Before bed, I give the boys back rubs, talking to them about their week.

After church on Sabbath, we try to spend family time together— either inviting friends over, going for a hike or a bike ride, or visiting grandparents. We attempt to make the day different than any other day of the week, a day to look forward to.

Another "rule" we've made is that Tim and I will have a date night once a month. This rule gets broken more often than any other. We didn't make the rule just to add another thing to the list of things we had to do. We want to spend time together. To go out. To get away from everything. To have fun and relax and talk. We know it's important for our marriage.

We also limit how many activities the boys can be involved in. It's important for our children to be involved in extra curricular activities. Kids who are involved in a variety of activities do better in school and stay out of trouble more often. But many of today's kids are over-involved, setting a pattern for their future lives. We can help them find balance later by teaching them how to find it now. Talk with your kids about all the things they're involved in and limit the number. Let them pick one extracurricular activity each season. Limit the number of hours they work at a part-time job during the school year. Teach them good habits such as getting to bed early. Remember that you're the parent; it's up to you to teach your children lessons that will lay the foundation for a balanced life. God has given you that responsibility. Sometimes, in an effort to not make our kids mad at us, or because it takes effort and time, we let our kids make their own choices without guiding them. Set boundaries. Help them to learn the tools necessary for making good decisions.

4. Plan quality time. Our family and friends need quantity time. But they also need quality time. Times that can become memory-makers. Think about what your family members enjoy doing and do it with them. Josh taught me how to roller blade. He's shown me how to do tricks on the skateboard—though I haven't given them a try! I've ridden go-carts with both boys. Shared a favorite restaurant of mine with Josh. Taken Zack to the Humane League more times than I can count. Tim and I have gone miniature golfing. We love to spend the day hiking or at a favorite farmers' market. We take the whole family camping or biking or sometimes canoeing. My mom and I take a whole day once in a while to go shopping together, even if we don't buy anything. We spend the day eating lunch out, catching up. I do the same things with friends. Right now, my friend, Lilly, has invited me to have tea with her at a tea room. We're both looking forward to getting away for a couple of hours—just the two of us—to talk and catch up with no interruptions.

What makes for quality time? A chance to talk. To really open up and share with each other. A time to get to know each other better. The dictionary's definition of quality is "how good something is." Quality time, then, would be good time together. Fun time. Time to draw closer to each other.

Quality time usually means time that we've set aside to spend with each other. A date night with our kids or spouse. A ladies night out with friends. A family dinner to get together with extended family. We can schedule it into our calendars and make it a regular event. Quality time can be Dad taking a different kid out to breakfast once a month. They won't forget who's turn it is. Tim did this years ago with the boys, and they still remember those mornings at a local diner. Or quality time can be a special, one-time event. This year, Tim wants to take each boy, separately, for a weekend camping. He's occasionally gone with his brother or a friend on a camping trip to New England. I encourage him to take these weekends. He comes home relaxed and in a better mood.

Schedule a trip to the library. Tanya takes her boys to a weekly story hour. Help your children choose books to read together; share your childhood favorites. Pick out a couple of books for yourself.

Plan a monthly date night with your spouse. Schedule a regular lunch appointment with your mom or a friend. Take a vacation for a week or a weekend or a day. Kidnap your husband from work for a surprise lunch. Try out that new skate park with your son. Take your daughter somewhere special on a "girls only" day. My sister-in-law, Shelly, and niece, Chelsea, stopped by the other day to see our kittens. They were on their way out for a "girls only" day, to shop, have ice cream, visit the kittens. At the same time, my brother and the boys were having a "guys only" day. Shelly said they plan these days often. Yet I know that they also do a lot of things together as a family. They camp often with my other brother and his family. Their kids, all the same ages, enjoy fishing. They set up their campers and head to the lake to fish.

Plan special time together—enjoyable time, opportunities to get to know each other better, to say, "I love you" by setting aside the time for things that your loved ones will enjoy. That's quality time.

5. *Have quantity time.* We can plan special moments, little surprises that make memories for a lifetime. And it's important that we do so. But we need to have quantity time as well. Quantity time includes those ordinary days when we're together, doing the things that we have to do—household chores, paying bills, running errands, eating dinner, just hanging out with nothing planned. But we're together. It's in these moments when life can be its most rewarding. When the joys of parenthood catch you by surprise as you watch your kids play or listen to them talk. Talking with a friend on the phone as you clean house—talking about anything and everything. Ordinary moments with your spouse working around the house.

Tim has been doing that a lot lately, building our new upstairs. There have been days that every time he passed me, he stopped and gave me a kiss. Evenings when I have sat on the scaffolding talking to him as he hung siding.

Spending quantity time may be difficult. With *quality* time, we can plan for it and schedule it—dates and vacations, for example. We can tuck these around all the other things we have to do and fill our schedules to the max. But quantity time isn't something we can schedule or plan, right?

Yes and No. Quantity time isn't something we necessarily plan. But we can schedule it in a sense—by *not* filling our schedule with something else. By freeing up our schedules, by not planning so many activities, we can help make sure there is simply more time for being with family and friends for the ordinary things of life. It seems obvious, but to have quantity time, we have to have time. Not free time. Not time when we have nothing to do; but an adequate amount of time when we can be together with others.

The good thing about quantity time is that it's also time when we can each be doing different things at the same time. Like Tim working on the house and me working on other things, bumping into each other, one of us being able to take a break and go talk to—or kiss—the other one. Quantity time is being around the house when our kids are home and being available for them to talk to.

We need both quality and quantity time. In order to have both, we need to realize how important they are. We need to understand what it costs us when they are missing in our lives. Having quality time and quantity time requires letting other things go. Not working late as often. Saying No to other good commitments in order to have time for the people we love. Finding balance means determining what is really important and putting it first. It means cutting out things that aren't as important, even if they are good things. It means assessing our goals in life. Do we need a huge house, a new car, the latest fashions? All these are nice, and by society's standards, important. Maybe even required. But in God's eyes, people have always been more important than things. They alone are lasting. We can live in such a way as to teach our children about God—not just the dos and don'ts, but how to live in such a way that we can have a relationship with God. We can help them to experience Him every day, every moment. But to do so we must live such a relationship in front of them. Sharing Him with them. Sharing the things He has taught us. Our lives can draw our children, spouses, and friends to God; but not if we don't have time for them.

How important are the people in your life? Important enough to say No to overtime at work? Which does your family need more— the money or time with you? Are the people in your life important enough to you to limit the number of things you're involved in at church and in your community? Do you have friends? Do you regularly schedule time for friends? Time is the only way to keep our relationships strong.

Thinking and Talking About It

1. For a week, keep a schedule of how you spend your time. How much time have you given your kids? Your spouse? Your friends? The results may surprise you.

2. How important are the people in your life? Does the time you spend with them reflect that importance? Do you need to make some changes?

3. What are the boundaries you've set for your family time? What rules can you make to protect those boundaries?

4. During the past few months, how have you spent quality time with your family and friends? Do you regularly schedule quality time? Take out your calendar and see where you can schedule time for dates or a vacation—even if it's a mini one.

5. Does your family have quantity time—large amounts of time to hang out together, even if everyone is home doing chores? Are there things you can cancel from your schedule in order to have at least two or three evenings a week at home together? This may require the entire family sitting down with their calendars. Plan a dinner to go over your calendars together.

CHAPTER SEVEN

You're Either Born With It or You Learn It

I believe that either you're born organized or you're not. If you're not, you can learn organizational skills, but staying organized will always seem more like work than second nature. Personally, I love to organize—anything, anybody. I love putting things together and having things in place and in order. My downfall is that I can be obsessive about it. I can't stand things out of place. I notice when a picture is hanging slightly crooked. Or when the pillows on the sofa are out of place. I enjoyed Nancy Van Pelt's book, *Getting Organized*. To me, it was just common sense. But if organization isn't your thing, you might better enjoy Beverly Graham Stickle's books, *Slow Down and Simplify* and *Hospitality on a Wing and A Prayer*.

Organization and boundaries can help you find balance and make your life easier. It might take a little work to get organized to begin with, but it will be worth it in the long run. The key is to *stay* organized. Once you have your home organized, keep it that way.

Start slow. Set aside an hour a week or half an hour a day—whatever you can schedule. You'll be surprised how much you can accomplish in an hour and how good it will feel.

There are a lot of great books on how to organize your entire life and home. That isn't what this chapter is about. We'll focus on ways to organize our homes and lives to help us find balance and time. Here are some things that have helped me:

1. The kitchen. Plan your menus in advance. The simplest way is to make a meal schedule for a month and then just use it again each month. I plan about a week in advance. My meal plan is flexible. I'll skip what is planned and fix something else if the mood strikes or serve a leftover potluck, much to the dismay of my family. Planning your meals saves the frustration of trying to decide at the end of a busy day what to fix for dinner.

I keep a grocery list in a central place in my kitchen. Every time anyone uses up an item or we are getting low, he writes it down. (OK, every time *I* use something up or see we are getting low, *I* write it down. The guys sometimes do. We're trying.)

Grocery shop only once a week or once every other week. I try to limit grocery stops in between. I always end up buying more than just the item or items I needed. I grocery shop every other week for the main things. On the off week, I pick up fresh vegetables, milk, and anything we need that can't wait until the next week. In our area, there is a "bump and banged" grocery store. Everything is much cheaper, but it's a little banged up. The store is always so crowded that it takes forever to get through the store and check out.

So I go there only once every other week. Some people, who have to drive a bit farther than I do, shop there only once a month. I don't have the storage area to shop only once a month.

When I put things away, I take the time to make sure everything is stacked in the cupboards in a way that I can see the labels easily. Also, all the canned goods go in one cupboard. Cereals go together—usually in see-through storage containers so I can see how much there is at a glance. Pastas go together in another cupboard. Taking the time to put things together and in such a way that you can see what you have at a glance will save time when it is time to cook, plan meals, or make a grocery list.

I've purchased inexpensive, plastic storage baskets for the kitchen, too. I use them in cupboards to store small things such as lids, plastic containers, and water bottles. The baskets keep everything organized, and when I need something, I just pull out the basket and find what I want. Smaller baskets help to sort odds and ends in drawers.

I also keep a pretty woven basket on the counter for small items. Things that are left on the counter can be dropped in the basket to keep the counter top clutter free.

2. Calendar. My calendar hangs in the kitchen by the phone. All the family's activities are written on it. At the beginning of the year, I mark significant birthdays on it. My mother-in-law gave me a birthday book. I keep birthdays updated in it but write them on the calendar at the beginning of each year. I would never remember to look in the book, yet it's a handy place to keep all the birthdays listed. Dinner ideas go on the calendar in red ink. That is the only thing written in red. It causes the meals to stand out so I can see in a glance what I'm making for dinner that night.

Because I keep track of everything on the calendar, I like one with big spaces. Lately I've added a wipe-off board on the refrigerator to remind me of daily "to do" items that I wouldn't write on the calendar—little things that I want to remember, such as phone calls, bills that need to be paid, chores for the boys. That way, I can see my week in a glance and cross off things as they are done.

Writing everything on a calendar that is out where you will see it every day will keep you from forgetting things. Writing on the wipe off calendar helps me, too. Often it's the little details that I forget. Writing them down when I think of them helps me to not forget them when I need to remember.

I also carry a day planner. When I go to meetings or to the doctor or dentist or orthodontist, I can easily schedule the next appointment or meeting. Having the day planner with me also gives me a place to write things down as they come to my mind during the day. If I need to remember to send out an information packet next week, I write it on the day I need to do it. Too many times I think about something I want to do, then forget it when the time comes. Writing it down when I think of it helps me to not forget. (You just have to remember to look in the planner or on the calendar.)

It's helpful to write in your schedule not only things you *have* to do, but things you *want* to do. Dates with your mate. Play times with your children (or someone else's.) Time with friends. Even time just to do those things *you* want to do—read, work on a hobby, go for a walk. Big chores that need to be done only once in awhile, I write in my weekly planner. Right now, my days have "WRITE" noted across them in big letters!

But to make all this work, you have to guard your time. When someone calls wanting you to do something, it's OK to tell them, "I have something else planned for that time, how about . . ." and pick another time that suits you. You don't have to tell them what is scheduled. And don't feel guilty for putting someone off in order to do something that is really important to you. Even if it is just taking time to sit and read that book you've been wanting to read.

Before adding anything to my schedule, I try to do two things. First, I pray about it. Is it something that God wants me to do? Then I ask myself how it fits with my priorities. If it is something God wants me to do, I'll do it, no matter what it is. But checking my priorities often reminds me of how I really want to spend my time and that although some things may not fit into my schedule, they do fit with my priorities and what I want my life to be. Like the morning the school teacher called. "Can you come in today and sub?" she asked. "The aide is sick and won't be able to make it."

We were all getting ready for the day. I would soon be on the road to take the boys to school, then headed home to start my long to–do list. I had already put off getting to the list for a couple of days, and it was only getting longer. The teacher's request wasn't going to make it any shorter. Inwardly I groaned. Another delay in my plans. But I also knew that I had made a commitment to myself to be there for the teacher and school in whatever way I could. So I said Yes and rescheduled everything mentally for another time. I hated putting everything off again, but I knew that it was the right thing to do. People are more important than accomplishing a to–do list. And I believed it was what God wanted me to do.

I've seen Him use my "sacrifice" of time for His benefit. One afternoon I received a note from one of the girls at school. She thanked me for always being willing to give up what I wanted to do to help them. She told me that I made it fun. Her note is a treasure, a reminder that what God sees as a significant accomplishment may be different than what the world considers an accomplishment. And with God, accomplishments last for eternity.

3. Delegate responsibility. I grew up in a very traditional home. Dad worked a full-time job and sometimes an extra part-time job. He took care of the car and the yard. Mom stayed home and took care of everything else around the house and was responsible for all five of us children. She made all the beds except mine. She put away the boys' laundry and fixed all the meals from things she had grown in the garden or picked off the fruit trees or bushes across the road and then canned or froze. Being the only girl, I had to help with the dishes and dust furniture. I also had to make my own bed and put away my own laundry. The boys didn't have to help in the house at all. They helped with the outside chores. Our teen years were spent on a mini-farm, so there were animals to feed, land to clear (somehow I had to help with that, too), and machinery to work on. Tim grew up in a traditional home, too. So our lives together seemed to fall automatically into the same pattern. In the beginning, we both had jobs outside the home. But on weekends and evenings, I took care of the house; he worked on the car or in the yard.

As the boys have grown older, I have decided that they can help around the house. Some of you may wonder why it took me so long to make that decision. I want the boys to learn to be responsible for their own things. So we have set up a little system that they hate. Many of their friends receive an allowance. They thought they should, too. I decided it would be good for them to have a little money so they could learn to save and to spend, but I didn't want to just give them money for no reason. So I made a list of the things I expected them to do. Simple things such as making their beds, putting their dirty clothes in the hamper, putting clean clothes away neatly, keeping their closets clean, and mowing the yard. Each job has a value. For instance, making the bed is twenty-five cents. If they do all their chores, they receive $5.00 a week in allowance. (Yes, the chores do add up to more than $5.00, but that is what we have budgeted.) If they don't do something on the list, that amount gets deducted from their allowance. This morning I gave them each their allowance for the week. It was a tough week. Zack got seventy-five cents—a reflection of how little he likes to help. Josh always does more; he is older and more responsible. My goal is not to see how little I can give them each week but to encourage them to be responsible for their own things. They need to learn these skills.

They also have chores not on the list and for which they are not paid. Nothing major. Occasionally they will wash all the dishes. Usually they just wash their own place setting. I wash dishes as I cook dinner, so that by the time we sit down, all the dishes are pretty much washed except what is on the table. I run water when I begin to prepare dinner, and while things are cooking, I wash what I've used. I hate long evenings in the kitchen after supper!

I may also ask the boys to sweep the floor, dust, vacuum, wipe out the window sills (living in the woods, we have a lot of spiders), or sweep the sidewalks. I'm trying to teach them that we are all a part of this family. It's our home, and we each need to help out and do our part. We are a team.

Zack doesn't like to work, so he will often whine or ask, "Why do I have to?"

I just answer, "Why not?" And if he whines about having to do something, I let him know that if he continues to whine, I'll give him another job to do. I may be tough, but I want very much for my boys to grow up with the habit of helping around the house and being responsible for their things. I think their wives will appreciate it someday.

Before the kids go to bed, have them pick up and put away all their toys—not just "put away," as Zack likes to do, but put away where they belong. In the morning, remind them to make their beds. I've made sure the beds are simple to make—a comforter is easy for a child to pull up, and even if the sheets underneath aren't completely wrinkle free, the bed looks nice. Teach them at an early age to pick up—to put their dirty clothes in the hamper, to hang up their towels and wash cloths after a bath. Reward them with words of encouragement. When the boys were very young, we would literally applaud the things they did and cheer them on. It boosted their egos and encouraged them to do it again.

When delegating jobs to your kids, take into consideration their age and abilities. Doing jobs all together often helps make it more fun. I make lists of jobs—one column with large jobs, one with small. Each of us chooses a chore from the large-job column and then we work at the same time to get our part done. Then we each choose a small job. It never takes long to get everything done that way. Then the boys are rewarded with some time to play with Mom.

And don't forget to enlist the help of your spouse. Sometimes he just needs to be asked. Let him help. Ask him to help. Give him something specific to do. Or offer him a couple of choices. The family is a team. Sometimes we need to work on remembering that.

4. Everything has a place. I like everything in its place. But it has to have a place first. I attempt to organize clothes closets with pants, shirts, and dresses, etc., together. I can usually keep my closet that way, and it makes everything easier to find. But it's harder keeping the guys' closets that way. I try. (They are usually the ones who can't find something.)

Shoe boxes or the plastic organizers available at department stores help in organizing drawers, especially for small things. These help the boys to keep things where they belong. A shoebox fits into their drawers nicely—one for underwear, one for socks, one for miscellaneous items. (They have a lot of miscellaneous!) I usually give each boy a "treasure" drawer that I never look in—for all those wonderful things they just have to keep.

For my desk or computer table, I have a basket for odds and ends, containers for paper clips, pens, and rubber bands, a plastic divider for papers, and colored cardboard folders for the different responsibilities I have. When there is something I need to remember to do or respond to, I just pull that folder. In the church folder, I keep a current membership list. In the writing folder are my thoughts and articles I want to use. One folder is for receipts I need to turn in. There is a basket for bills that need to be paid. A filing cabinet holds all the receipts for things that have already been paid—filed by categories so they are easy to find come tax time.

Once everything has a place, make sure it goes there whenever it's not being used. Too many times, things get laid somewhere with the intention of being put away later, but they are left to lie there until they are needed again. Then the item is not where it belongs, and you can't find it when you need it. It doesn't take long to put something away—right away. Teach family members to do the same.

5. *Mail.* I used to love getting mail. I love letters from friends. These days, most personal letters come via e-mail. And regular mail is mostly bills or junk. Go through your mail when you get it, and put it where it belongs as you sort it. Junk mail goes in the trash. Bills to be paid go in my basket. If the piece is for one of the ministries I'm working with, it goes in that folder. Any mail Tim needs to see goes by his plate at the dinner table. That pile can pile up. So after supper, or the next morning while I'm packing lunches and getting breakfast together, I go through it and trash what he isn't interested in and put the rest where it belongs.

6. *Routine.* A daily or weekly routine helps you stay organized too. Many of our mothers or grandmothers had a weekly routine. One day was always wash day—and it took all day. Another day might have been baking day. Today, we head off to work most days. But we can still have a routine.

Starting the day at the same time each day is a good beginning. I like to get up, pack Tim's lunch, feed the cats, and have my quiet time. While everyone is still sleeping (hopefully), I head out for my walk. Back home, I exercise, take a shower, and then begin the process of waking everyone up for their turn in the bathroom. After breakfast, Tim heads to work, and the boys and I head to school. Monday, Wednesday, and Friday are my days at home—to write, do housework or laundry, and take care of the things in the folders. Tuesday and Thursday are my days out. Tuesday I grocery shop. During the summer, when the boys are out of school, we pick up my granny and take her with us for the day. During the school year, I shop and attend the Bible study at church with the mother's group. Thursday, I pray with my prayer partner. During the school year, I volunteer at the school to serve as the PE teacher during morning recess. Tuesday and Thursday are the two days that work best for me to squeeze in time with friends or fun things—like a trip to the mall or Roots' Market. I'm already out, so I attempt to run all my errands on these days.

After school, there is homework. Dinner. Reading a book together or playing a game. Baths and bedtime. The boys are in bed early so that Tim and I can have some time together and still be in bed early enough to get a good night's sleep. If I stay up late too many nights, I can't wake up early in the morning. And that throws off my routine. I've promised myself to have my quiet time and exercise before starting anything else, so if I get up late, I get a very late start on my to do list. That is frustrating to me. So I like to start early.

During the summer, when there is no school, the boys would love to play the whole day. But after breakfast, Zack has to work on a couple of pages from his math book, and I give them each a chore or two do. After lunch, we set the timer and each of us finds a cozy spot to read for half an hour. Before supper, I assign another chore.

None of our routine is rigid. If something comes up, we're flexible. But having a routine helps keep us organized and ensures that we have time to do what needs to be done. Without planning, nothing may get done. Or it may get put off to another day. Planning ahead makes it more likely you will be able to do all you need to get done.

You may want to include a cleaning routine. If it's difficult to get the whole house clean in one day, assign different jobs for each day, so that by the end of the week the whole house has been cleaned. Because my days are flexible, I clean on Fridays, although I spot clean throughout the week. I like the house to be totally clean by Sabbath. It helps me to relax more. But if you work all day, it is impossible to get all your cleaning done in one evening unless it is a family project and everyone pitches in with a chore or two.

It is possible to organize your home and calendar but still have clutter in your life. Being organized—having an organized house or week—won't cause you to be balanced, but it will make the process of balancing easier. And we need all we can find to make life easier.

Thinking and Talking About It

1. How organized are you? How organized do you want to be?

2. Do you think organization could help make your life a little easier?

3. How much time can you commit each day or week to begin getting organized?

4. Make a plan of where you want to begin—with a room, your

calendar, your routine, delegating, etc.—and begin the process. Begin with a drawer. A closet. Buy a calendar. Make up a chart or chores to do. You may want to read Nancy Van Pelt's, *Getting Organized* or Beverly Graham Stickle's *Hospitality on a Wing and a Prayer* or Emilie Barnes's *Survival for Busy Women.*

5. Talk to friends and find out what organizational tips have helped them the most.

CHAPTER EIGHT

What About Me?

Work. Church. Community. Home. Family. Friends. There are so many demands on our time and energies, and all of them are important. What is usually the first thing to go from our over-crowded schedules—if it was even there in the first place?

Time for ourselves. There is often more than one reason for this.

We are busy. The urgent comes first, and time for ourselves rarely seems urgent.

We think we can handle it. We're super moms, super women. Aren't we supposed to be able to do it all—without complaining, of course?

We don't want to be selfish. Many of us think that taking time for ourselves is selfish. That it is putting ourselves first before other things that need to be done. And how can we do that?

I'm learning that the real question is, How can we not? How can we keep giving and giving, running and running, and eventually not give up or run out? "When you give more than you have, you burn out. . . . You have to keep replenishing" (Walter Pierson, Jr, *Ministry Downlink*, April 20, 1999).

Taking care of myself isn't just for me. When I'm replenished, I have more to give. When I burn out, I have nothing. I'm irritable, grouchy, and snap easily. I'm not the kind of mom or friend I want to be. If I want to give, I must have something to give away. I have to take time for myself in order to serve others. That isn't selfish. It's basic supply and demand. You have to have supply to meet the demand.

Sometimes when it feels that I'm doing all the giving, I begin to resent it. I get tired of having to keep doing and doing, giving and giving. I begin to wonder, "Who is giving back to *me?*" I don't do things for others so that they will give something back to me. But when I continue to pour out myself into other things and people, without putting anything back, I feel empty and tired, exhausted and worn out. And I just want someone to take care of me for a change.

When I'm on the verge of burning out completely, I begin thinking, "Why can't someone else help out around here? Why do I always have to be the one to do this?" I get angry—at Tim, at the boys, at others. Most of the time, my anger is irrational. I'm the one who has put many of these demands on myself. Or at least, I'm the one who has accepted them. I know that if I need to be taken care of, that I need to do it.

Women are used to taking care of everyone else, but we are lousy at taking care of ourselves. We fix our families healthful meals but eat on the run ourselves, usually grabbing junk. We make our children go to bed early and get plenty of sleep, but we stay up late trying to get everything done. Then we get up early to take care of everyone. We do little things to show others we love them—sending cards, making favorite meals, running here and there. Then we fall into bed at night wondering when it is going to be our turn and feeling guilty that we are even thinking about ourselves.

When I first started staying home full-time with a baby, I would wait all day for Tim to come home. When he arrived, I thought he would take care of all my wants and needs. I thought he would supply me with enough adult conversation to last me through the next day. I thought he would take care of the baby so I could have a break. I often wanted to go somewhere and do something after being home all day. He just wanted to stay home; he was tired of being out. And he didn't want to talk. He had talked enough during the day. After a few weeks or months of feeling sorry for myself and being angry at him, I realized that I couldn't expect him to take care of my needs. He didn't even know most of them. (It didn't help that I never told him specifically what I needed; I just expected him to know.) I realized that if I wanted my needs met, I needed to make sure they were met. I couldn't expect Tim or anyone else to do it for me. I could take my needs to God. And I could take care of myself.

As I approach forty (and it's coming faster than I'd like to think), I've also realized the need to take care of myself physically. The pounds are easier to put on and harder to take off. Life seems to get busier and more stressful everyday. Lilly and I were talking about how busy we thought our lives were a few years ago when our boys were younger. We struggled even then to fit everything in. Yet we had time to write notes and to get together occasionally. Compared to today, life was more simple, easier, less stressful. It's harder to get together or write that occasional note. Even an e-mail once in awhile becomes hard to squeeze in. Life continues to pick up speed, and too often I feel that I'm not in control.

But I'm learning to take care of me. I'm realizing that by taking care of me, I'm enabling myself to take better care of others. I'm more patient and less frustrated. I don't feel as stressed. The most important thing I'm doing for myself is spending time with God. I'm focusing on my relationship with Him and growing in Him. I do that for me. As I grow in Him, I have more peace. I can trust Him no matter how much my world spins out of control—and at times it spins wildly, threatening to overwhelm me completely. But as I focus on Him, everything else comes into focus.

I've made my quiet time with Him a priority. But it is no longer a method or formula—a list of things to do. Something to check off my list. It's a relationship with a Father who I know loves me.

How do I know He loves *me?* Faulty, sinful, over-committed, forgetting-Him-at-times me?

His Word tells me. And I read His Word, studying it so that I can know Him. I've memorized scriptures that remind me that He loves and cares for me. I keep my praise journal—a constant reminder of the things God is doing in my life for which I can be thankful. In the Bible He constantly told His people to remember how He had led them in the past—and to tell their children and to remind each other. Remembering what God has done for us, how He has led us, encourages us now. It reminds us that God has taken care of us before and that He will take care of us today—no matter what.

The Bible stories themselves are an encouragement to me as I look at people such as David, Peter, and Abraham and how they struggled and failed God, yet He still counted them as His people. He didn't tell David that he could no longer be king after committing adultery and having Bathsheba's husband killed in battled. He called David a man after His own heart. He didn't walk away from Peter when Peter denied Him three times—after proudly boasting that he would never leave Him and would die for Him. He gave Peter an opportunity to be reconciled and then gave him a mission. Abraham and Sarah believed God would keep His promises. But when it didn't happen according to their timing, they "helped" God—and ended up causing a lot of problems. Yet God still fulfilled His promise and blessed them. He counted their belief as faith even when they doubted and tried to help. As I read these stories, looking for God in them, I'm reminded that even when I sin, even when I fail God or try to "help" Him, God still loves me. He still works in and through me.

Spending time with God is one of my priorities. But it is also something I do for me. And God uses these moments, this time of teaching me and talking to me, to bless others. He gives me lessons and ideas to share with others. He helps me to encourage them. The Samaritan woman had an encounter with Jesus (see John 4). He encouraged her, spoke to her, and met her needs. She immediately shared Him with her village, and an entire village came to hear Him, believed on Him, and claimed Him as Savior. If she hadn't spent that time with Jesus, an entire village would have missed out on knowing Him. Who misses out when I don't spend time with Jesus?

The women's Bible study of which I'm a part is another thing I do for me. This monthly commitment gets me together with other women who are searching for a more intimate relationship with God, for purpose, for balance. We talk. Share from our lives. We share what God taught us through the lessons. These times are important, not just for the study, but for the sharing. For the opportunity to pray with one another about the deepest needs in our hearts. I go away most weeks feeling encouraged and stronger—that I'm not alone. Occasionally, a couple of us will go out for lunch afterwards; we don't want that time to end.

Friendship is important to me. So time with friends is something else I do for me. It's a way of taking care of me. Friends bring me strength and encouragement. They give me someone to turn to when times are tough and someone to share with when things are exciting. We laugh together. Talk. Share. Cry together. Time with friends is hard to squeeze in. But we can talk on the phone while we cook or clean. (My telephone line reaches all over the house, and for Christmas, my brother-in-law bought me a cordless phone.) Time for friends can include an occasional lunch out, an outing to the craft show, working on projects at church or school together, celebrating special moments (like Ann's fortieth birthday), or just hanging out once in a while in the back yard, watching the kids play, and talking.

This year I made a new commitment to myself to exercise on a regular basis. Each morning, I head out at a brisk pace around our country block. When I get home, I do some crunches and leg lifts while I catch the morning news. It has meant cramming something else into an already busy morning, but for me, it's worth it. It means getting up a little earlier. It means staying committed to getting up and moving, or else I'm going to fall behind schedule. I've also learned that on those few mornings when something does happen and I don't have time to fit in the entire morning routine, I can either exercise later in the day, or put it off till the next day without feeling guilty. By trying to do it every morning, I'm able to exercise at least four or five times a week. That's a plus. It's more than I was doing before. And I can see the difference. I feel better. Sleep better. Fit into my clothes better. And I think I have a better, more upbeat, attitude. But exercise is not a requirement that I have to meet in order to keep the day from being a total failure. Exercise, eating healthy, and getting enough sleep is something I want to do. But I'm still an OK person if I miss a day.

That concept is an important one—not only to realize but to live. We need to understand that although we may have things we want to do, they aren't what defines us. They are just things we would like to accomplish each day. If we don't get them done, it's OK. We're OK. Not failures. Not worthless. Just people who are trying to grow and learn and be the best people we can be. If I grab a candy bar instead of a salad, if I don't get the house cleaned, if I miss my morning walk, or if I serve dinner on paper plates because

I don't feel like doing the dishes, it's OK. The world won't end. I'm still me. I'm me because of who I am on the inside not because of what I do or don't do on the outside.

A lot of what I do for me may not even seem like it is for me—quiet time with God, exercise, Bible study. But each of these things helps me to feel better. Brings me encouragement. Gives me a sense of balance. But there are other things I do that are a bit more just for me.

Hobbies, for example. One of my favorite things when I have free time is to read. I love books! I enjoy snuggling up with a book and a cup of cocoa on a cool night or just sitting quietly for a few minutes reading. I also enjoy listening to music. I love to be able to listen to a song without any interruptions—singing along, dancing around the house.

Occasionally I take a day off. Once in a while I need to get away from it all. Since I don't have a job outside the home, it's hard to get away from work. When I'm home, the phone still rings, and I can see all the things I should be doing. So although sometimes I will take a day off at home—usually to read, study my Bible, or pray—I often go out when I take a day off. Both types of "retreat" are helpful. This past spring I took a day off at home to read and pray through Stormie Omartian's, *The Power of a Praying Wife*. That's what I did all day—read and prayed and relaxed. I learned to pray for Tim about things I had never thought of before.

I'm looking forward to the boys going back to school so I can take a Tuesday off to spend at Roots' Market. Roots' is a huge farmers' market with stand after stand of fresh produce, flowers, baked goods, and crafts. There is also a flea market where I hunt for pretty or unusual tea cups and tea pots. I enjoy the smells and watching people—buying little, but enjoying it all.

Take a day off to go over your calendar and commitments. To pray about what God wants in your schedule and days. How does He want you to spend your time? Are there changes that you need to make? How do you begin making those changes and start taking time to replenish yourself? How do you do things you enjoy doing?

Schedule time to go places you've always wanted to go but never have had a chance. Take a day off to become a tourist in your own back yard. Spend the day at the mall. (Though I've found that isn't fun for me unless I have a friend along.) Treat yourself to lunch at your favorite restaurant or try a new place. Linger over the meal, enjoying a magazine or book or just sitting quietly. Relax in a bubble bath with candles and your favorite music. Set the timer after lunch or dinner and read for half an hour. Get your kids reading, too. Take your sneakers to work with you and walk briskly around the block after lunch. Go to a garden somewhere and stroll through the flowers. In our area, beautiful Longwood Gardens has incredible flower displays all year—rose gardens in the summer; poinsettias in the winter; spring flowers that are bright with color. Tim and I spent a cold winter afternoon there before Christmas the other year. It's a memory that I'd love to repeat! We listened to the Christmas carols played on a huge organ. Saw the light display after dark. Ate vegetarian chili and cornbread by the huge windows overlooking the gardens.

I'm learning that everything on my schedule doesn't have to be done today. Some of it can wait. I'm attempting to put off till tomorrow what can wait. To not fill my day too full and to leave room for those unexpected moments God brings—a phone call from a friend, time to sit and talk with one of the kids, a nap, a chance to write a note and catch up on a friendship. I think a workaholic must have started the saying, "Don't put off till tomorrow what can be done today." If it can wait and you need it to, let it. That doesn't mean I'm letting things go. I'm still getting things done. But accomplishing a to do list isn't my top priority. My priority is to live each day the way God wants. I think He wants us to take breaks. To rest. To not run all day until we drop at night.

Time to get away refreshes us. It gives us that break—that time to breathe and regroup—that we need in our hectic lives. We need to include time for ourselves in our schedules. We need to realize that such time is important for our health and that replenishing ourselves enables us to have more to give to others. God never intended us to run on empty. He created the world for us to enjoy—not to rush past never seeing the color of flowers, the majesty of mountains, the calming effect of waters. And I think He must love books; He gave us one to read and reread. He knew that it wasn't good for us to be alone, so He created spouses and gave us families. He told us to encourage one another and to love one another. I believe He wants us to take care of ourselves—for Him and for those He has given us to love. I think He longs for us to take the time to laugh and talk with our kids so that when they need us, they will know we are there. I believe God longs for our marriages to be a deepening friendship, growing every day in the time we spend together. I think He wants more for us than work.

How would God plan our day if He could sit down with our day planners and fill in all the lines?

I asked a group of women that question one day. We agreed that God would definitely schedule time with Him. He would also want us to take time for the important people in our lives—family and friends. We believed that He would schedule work for us to do. God wouldn't want us just to hang out or lay around and be lazy everyday. He created us with the ability to do things—to work, to provide for ourselves and our families. But we also decided that God would schedule time for us. Time for us to take care of ourselves. To relax and enjoy this life that He has given us. He wants us to have joy—not drudgery—everyday. He promises us rest, not constant busyness. He loves us and wants the best for us.

Thinking and Talking About It

1. What do you do each day/week/month for yourself? How much time to do you schedule in your calendar for you? Are you setting aside time for yourself on a regular basis?

2. If you don't set aside time for yourself, why not? Does not having time for yourself affect you in anyway—cause frustration, anger, resentment, etc.?

3. If God could take your calendar and plan each day for you, what kinds of things do you think He would include? Do you include these things?

4. What would it take to include time for yourself in your schedule on a regular, or semi-regular, basis?

CHAPTER NINE

Learning to Stand Still

"Be still, and know that I *am* God" (Psalm 46:10, NKJV).

It's hard for me to be still. I have this push to always be doing something. I don't even like to sit still. If I'm sitting, I'm reading, working on something, or fidgeting. When I watch TV, I'm usually doing something else, too; I rarely just sit and watch. I exercise. I iron. I read. All while keep tracking of what is happening on the tube. I hate just to be still!

Yet God has called us to be still. To stop all that we are doing. To close our mouths and open our ears. To know Him.

I've heard this verse often—"Be still, and know that I *am* God" (Psalm 46:10, NKJV). I have it underlined in my Bible with a note in the margin: "Close your mouth. Bend your knees, and *know* God. Listen. Watch." I thought I understood what this verse meant. I always related it to my devotional time. I felt it was telling me that at some point during my quiet time each day, I needed to stop praying and studying and just listen for God's voice. It was hard. By the time I finished all I had to say and do, there wasn't a lot of time left to listen for God's voice. And I wasn't sure what I was listening for, anyway. Would God's voice be audible? What would He say to me? Would He give me some kind of directive? As I tried to let my mind be quiet, a million thoughts threatened to overtake the stillness. My thoughts began reviewing all that I needed to do or replaying conversations or working on things in my mind. I'm not sure my brain is capable of being still or being without thoughts. Trying to be still before God seemed futile, impossible, frustrating.

Yet I wanted the promise that went along with being still. I wanted to know God.

God never yells. He won't yell over the chaos in our lives. I believe He does want us to stop and listen for His voice as we spend time with Him. He will attempt to get our attention. But we have to be quiet and listen for His voice. Yet I've found that there is more to being still than being quiet.

What does it mean to be still before God? How can I be still and yet be so busy? The phrase, "don't just stand there, do something" is part of my life. But God says, "Don't do anything, just stand there." He has said it several times, sometimes in very difficult situations.

I found the idea of being still in one of my favorite Bible stories. It doesn't say, "be still"; it says, "stand still." But it's the same thing as being still. God told the Israelites to " 'Stand still, and see the salvation of the Lord' " (Exodus 14:13, NKJV). The Red Sea was before them—an impenetrable wall of water. The Egyptian army was fast closing in on them from behind. If I were them, I'd want to run. Scatter. Get away. (That is how I feel sometimes when all the demands come closing in on me—I want to run away.) Yet God told the Israelites to stand still. Not to run. Not to try to find their own way out. Just stand still and watch Him. He parted the sea. He destroyed their enemy. He protected them and got them to safety.

Later, He told the priests to carry the ark of the covenant into the Jordan River and stand still (see Joshua 3:8). They were to stand still in the rushing water and let it swirl around their ankles. What they needed to do was to get to the other side. Standing still in the shallow water along the riverbank didn't look as though it was going to get them anywhere. Yet God told them to just wade in and stand there. To stand still. When they did, He parted the Jordan River. And as long as they stood still, the people could pass through safely to the other side.

My favorite story about being still is in 2 Chronicles 20. The children of Judah were afraid. Their enemies outnumbered them and had them surrounded. They didn't know what to do. " 'We have no power against this great multitude that is coming against us,' " they told God, " 'nor do we know what to do, but our eyes *are* upon You' " (verse 12, NKJV). Get the picture. The enemy is closing in for battle. God's children know they can't win; they aren't strong enough. They don't know where to begin—just as, many times, I don't. I just can't do it all. I don't even know where to begin. And through His prophet, God told them, " 'Do not be afraid nor dismayed because of this great multitude, for the battle *is* not yours, but God's. . . . You will not *need* to fight in this *battle*. Position yourselves, *stand still* and see the salvation of the Lord, who is with you' " (verses 15, 17, NKJV, emphasis supplied).

"Stand still. You may want to fight, to figure it out yourself, to do something. But don't. Just stand there and watch. I will fight this battle. It's Mine. I will save you." Everything in them cried out, "We've got to do something!" But God said, "Do nothing. Stand still." And God defeated their enemies—without His people doing a thing except singing praises to His name. It took them three days to collect all the spoils from the battle they didn't fight.

Stand still. Be still. Know that I am God.

How did they know He was God as they stood there?

Because they saw Him at work. They knew they weren't the ones doing it. They didn't part the Red Sea. They didn't cause the Jordan to dry up. They didn't defeat their enemies. They never drew their weapons in that battle. God had done it all.

And they came to know Him more. They knew that He was powerful. He could part the waters. They knew that He would protect them. He had defeated their enemies. They knew He loved them, that He would move the heavens and earth on their behalf.

There was another group of people who heard God's words, "Be still."

They were in a boat in the middle of a lake when a mighty storm blew in. Several of them were fishermen, yet they were afraid. The boat was filling with water faster than they could bail it out. It was rocking and tipping, and they didn't know what to do. They thought they were going to die. In panic, they called out to Jesus, asleep in the bow, " 'Teacher, do You not care that we are perishing?' " (Mark 4:38, NKJV). We're not going to make it! This storm is too much. The boat is rocking; our hope is sinking; and we are soaked with fear. Lord, help us!

Jesus arose and said to the wind and the waves, "Peace, be still." The storm stopped. The water was calm. The disciples started breathing again.

I think about these stories often. It seems like the storm rages in my life more often than I would like. At times, I don't know what to do. The enemy is closing in and is greater than I am. The storm is so frightening, so overwhelming. I feel that I need to be doing something, but I don't even know where to begin.

That is the kind of weekend I had recently. On top of all the day-to-day frustrations and living under construction, life seemed to explode with traumas. Thursday night, my brother had an accident at work causing him to lose a finger and parts of three more. Two days later, we received a call that my cousin's ten-year-old grandson was found dead—an accident while playing in a tree. Tim had a rough day with the construction on Sunday. The house was full of company all weekend—watching my brother's girls, my nephew spending the weekend, and celebrating Josh's birthday with grandparents. And on Friday, just as I was in the middle of fixing lunch for all five kids, the shutoff valve on a pipe upstairs came open and water streamed all over the place. It found a hole above the linen closet and cascaded down through all the sheets and blankets and on into the basement and where we had all kinds of things stored during the construction. It took me three hours to clean up the mess and hang out all the sheets to dry. Then I needed to take the girls to see their dad at the hospital, ending up an hour late to the birthday party to which I was supposed to take them. Monday morning at work, Tim's company experienced the worst accident it has ever had. An employee was critically injured. Being safety coordinator, Tim was responsible for filling out accident reports when no one even knew yet what had actually happened. Not a typical weekend, but the feeling of being overwhelmed with problems we can't control or fix can, all too often, be a way of life.

Things have a way of getting out of control—too many demands, more problems than you can handle. You just don't know where to turn or what to do. And often there isn't anything you can do. That is when God tells us to stand still. "Stand still, and know that I am God." When we can't handle it all, He can. When we aren't sure where to begin, He knows exactly how it will end. When there is nothing we can do, He can do it all. It's time to stand still.

But how do we stand still when life is storming all around us? When our already all-too-full lives explode with more problems?

1. Realize and admit that you just can't do it. God's children said, " 'we have no power . . . we do not know what to do' " (2 Chronicles 20:12, NIV). There are problems that we just can't do anything about. I couldn't fix my brother's hand. I couldn't fix the injured man at Tim's company or take away the intense grief my cousin's family was experiencing.

2. Look to God. "Our eyes are upon you" (verse 12). Give it to God. You may not know how to handle it, but He does. Turn to Him. Pray. Let Him know how you feel and what you need—your frustrations, your fears, your discouragement. He knows; He knows the answers. But He can't take care of your problems until you give them to Him. All I could do for those I cared about who were encountering traumas was to take them to Jesus. To pray. To trust that He would see them through. That He would bring healing and use the circumstances for His glory. I believe that God doesn't allow anything to happen to us for our harm. I believe that all that happens to us, even the terrible, God uses for our eternal good—to prepare us, grow us, make us the people He desires for us to be. I can say I believe it, but when faced with a real crisis, I have the opportunity to live it.

3. *Stand still.* " 'Do not be afraid nor dismayed. . . . Position yourselves, stand still and see the salvation of the Lord' " (verses 15, 17, NKJV). Let God take care of it. Give it to Him and let it go. Don't take it back. That is hard. We want to do something. We want to fix all the problems—even when we can't. Don't be afraid. Trust Him. Remind yourself of who He is.

How were the Israelites able to let go and stand still? They praised God. Praise turns our focus toward God and what He can do and who He is. Praise turns our focus off the problem and toward the only One who can take care of it. That's one way we can let go. Praise God. Focus on Him and not the problem. In my situation that hectic weekend, I praised God that He is a healer, that He can create miracles. I praised Him for being able to take a devastating situation and somehow use it for good. I thanked Him for being the God of all comfort and that He is the ultimate healer of people and relationships. Praising Him, focusing on who He is, brings me peace and assurance. I'm reminded that He is bigger than any problem I face and that He loves me with an overwhelming love.

Every time I'm tempted to start focusing on the problem, taking it back on my shoulders and throwing my life out of balance, I have to turn to Him again and refocus on Him and His ability to solve my problems. He is able. And even when things don't turn out as I would like, I can still live in the belief that He is in charge and knows what is best. Even when the end of the problem doesn't seem that evident, I can still believe that He is working and that the process is part of His plan.

How did the events of that traumatic weekend finally turn out?

The surgeons are amazed at my brother. His hand is doing better than they expected. He is one of the strongest men I know. And he has a sense of humor and a faith that will see him through this. I'm sure my cousin and her family will grieve their loss for a long time, but I trust God to wrap His arms around them. The man at work made it through the first twenty-four hours, a bit of a miracle itself. By the third day, he was holding his girlfriend's hand and smiling. The doctors believe he is going to make it. Josh enjoyed his birthday, and the house got back to "normal." Everything that got wet, dried, and nothing important was ruined. Through it all, I focused on a God who, I knew, didn't allow anything without supplying the grace and strength to get through it. I looked for His hand—His miracles—and found them. The supplies for an upcoming tea weren't touched by the water even though the container they were in had an inch of water on top of it. The box containing my wedding dress was soaked, but inside, the dress itself was untouched. Small things, but they reminded me of a big God who cares about even the tiniest of details of my life.

Sometimes our lives are out of balance because of all that we schedule into them. We may be able to reduce our workload, be more careful of our schedules, say No more often, and say Yes only to the things that are priorities. But sometimes, unexpected moments and tragedies throw everything off kilter. It is in those moments that we need to learn to stand still and see God at work. To admit that we can't and He can. To stand still and see Him as Lord of our lives while He takes care of all that matters to us.

Thinking and Talking About It

1. Are there things in your life that you can't control and that are throwing your life out of balance?

2. Are you trying to fix these things yourself? With any success?

3. Have you taken them to God? Have you left them there?

4. Are there any aspects of these problems about which you can praise God? (Remember that praise focuses on Him, not on the problem.)

5. What do you believe about God? Do you believe that He is intimately involved in your life and cares about even the smallest details? Do you believe that everything He allows to happen is ultimately for your good and that He doesn't allow bad things to happen just to punish or hurt you? Can you trust Him? Can you live it, not just say it?

CHAPTER TEN

Martha, Martha

"Now it happened as they went that He entered a certain village; and a certain woman named Martha welcomed Him into her house. And she had a sister called Mary, who also sat at Jesus' feet and heard His word. But Martha was distracted with much serving, and she approached Him and said, 'Lord, do You not care that my sister has left me to serve alone? Therefore tell her to help me.' And Jesus answered and said to her, 'Martha, Martha, you are worried and troubled about many things. But one thing is needed, and Mary has chosen that good part, which will not be taken away from her'" (Luke 10:38-42, NKJV).

I've felt like Martha many times. I've had women introduce themselves as a Martha. Martha's name seems to have become synonymous with serving and doing and working without much time for anything else. We read this story, and Martha ends up the bad guy. Mary is the "good" one. Some read the story and think that Jesus was reprimanding Martha, that He was telling her that Mary was right and she was wrong. That she needed to sit at His feet all the time. We Marthas know that can't be the case. If we all sat around, nothing would get done! Jesus definitely has a message for all the Marthas as much as for the Marys.

1. Jesus loved Martha. I was thrilled when I read John 11:5, "Now Jesus loved Martha and her sister and Lazarus" (NKJV). Jesus loved Martha. He knew her tendency to become distracted by all the things needing to be done. But He loved her. *The Desire of Ages* tells us that Jesus often found rest in the home of Martha and Lazarus; it was a place where He could get away and relax, where people came, who truly wanted to hear His words. Jesus not only loved Martha, but He enjoyed being in her home and visiting with her.

Jesus loves us, too—even when we're so busy doing that we're distracted. He enjoys visiting with us, talking to us. He wants to spend time with us.

2. Martha loved Jesus. She loved Him so much that she wanted everything to be perfect for Him—just the right food, a comfortable place to relax and eat. She cared about every detail. Serving was her way of showing love.

3. Martha sat at Jesus' feet too. Notice the little word "also" in Luke 10:39, "And she [Martha] had a sister called Mary, who *also* sat at Jesus' feet and heard His word" (NKJV, emphasis supplied). If Mary *also* sat, there must have been someone else that was sitting, too. This verse is introducing Mary in relation to Martha. Martha sat at Jesus' feet, too.

She listened to His words. She longed to know more.

But on this day, she wasn't sitting. She had a crowd of people in her home (Jesus had a group of at least twelve men who traveled with Him everywhere He went). She loved Jesus, and I think she got irritated with Mary because she was jealous that Mary was sitting and she wasn't. I believe that Martha wanted to be sitting, too— that she would rather be sitting than working. But the work needed to be done, didn't it? And if she didn't do it, who would? Mary?

So Martha went to Jesus and pointed out the problem. Like a child, she wanted Jesus to tell Mary to get up and help out. It wasn't fair; why should she have to do all the work while Mary enjoyed the company? Why did Mary get to listen?

Why didn't Martha just go ask Mary to help out? Why did she go to Jesus?

Maybe she needed that assurance that she was doing the right thing in serving. Isn't that what Jesus wants from us—service to Him? A lot of us ask that very question ourselves. Maybe we don't even realize that is what we think, but somewhere down inside we think that Jesus wants us to serve Him—all the time and in every way we can. So we say Yes to everything we are asked to do. We run, and we push. Isn't that what "good" Christians do? Isn't that our purpose? To serve?

Yes, and No.

God's will for us is that we have eternal life. That is why Jesus came to die—so that our sins could be forgiven and we could be with Him in heaven. He longs for us to be with Him. Heaven isn't heaven without us. But we can't get eternal life by serving. Eternal life is a gift we receive because we believe in Jesus and in the sacrifice He made for us. We can't do it on our own—can't earn it, can't inherit it from our parents. God's will is for us to know Him. He longs for a relationship with us. He gave everything He had so He could have us. Our service must come from our love for Him. It must be a result of the relationship we have with Him. Service is not the relationship. Service is not the mainstay. Service is not the most important thing. The most important thing is for us to know God—and not just know *about* Him, but to know Him. " 'And this is eternal life, that they may know You' " (John 17:3, NKJV). " 'And this is the will of Him who sent Me, that everyone who sees the Son and believes in Him may have everlasting life' " (John 6:40, NKJV). Jesus told the Samaritan woman that God desired people who would worship in spirit and truth (see John 4:23). He didn't say that God was looking for those who would worship Him in deeds. The deeds will come, but worship comes first.

That is what Jesus told Martha: " 'Martha, Martha, you are worried and troubled about many things' " (Luke 10:41, NKJV). The problem wasn't Martha's service; it was her focus. Martha was focused on all the things she needed to do. She was focused on doing it all and getting it right. She was "distracted with much serving" (verse 40). Her focus was on doing, not on Jesus. She wasn't thinking about Him or about what He wanted her to be doing. She was thinking about getting the meal on the table and the kitchen cleaned up.

" 'But one thing is needed, and Mary has chosen that good part' " (verse 42). One thing was needed—a focus change. What was Mary focused on? Jesus. She was sitting at His feet, listening to His words. Her eyes were on Jesus. Martha's eyes were on the job at hand.

What Mary learned in those moments at Jesus' feet could never be taken away from her, " '. . . which will not be taken away from her" (verse 42). Martha's meal would be eaten up. The clean house would become dirty again. The details she labored over would be lost on the men at the table. Mary would have something that would last forever. Martha would just be tired.

How like Martha my life often is! So focused on the doing. Attempting to keep up. To do it all. Rushing around and always feeling behind. Concentrating on what needs to be done. Missing those glorious moments when Jesus is speaking—through my children as they play and I rush around working; through the kittens who romp in the backyard while I hurry past to the car; through those quiet moments I'm too busy to take. Jesus is speaking, but I'm too busy listening to the voices asking me to do more, be more, give more. Until I just can't take it any more and drop it all.

That is the place I had come to. I had nothing left to give and a list of things yet to do, needs that had to be met, places I was supposed to go, people who were depending on me. Something had to give, and it couldn't be me. I had given it all I had to give.

That is how I began this journey of finding balance.

Many of my friends and I have discussed these issues. Tanya and I have sent e-mails back and forth about the multitude of demands on our time and on the need to find balance in our lives. We long to be there for our children, playing and teaching. But too often we are caught up in a race to get more done in one day than one day can hold. And the children end up with tired, frustrated moms who snap and who don't have time to play.

Sue and I pray about balance in my life. She learned the secret of a balanced life long before I did. It helps that her personality, unlike mine, doesn't enjoy being extremely busy. As I have watched her, I have learned to pace myself, too. Sue knows what God has called her to do, and that is what she does. She is a godly woman with many gifts who is asked to take on a myriad of things, but she has learned to focus on what is important and to do what God has called her to do. She has learned how to say No to all those great things she could do but which are not what God has asked her to do. When I first started seeing Sue say No, I couldn't believe it. Actually saying No! I admired it. I wanted that ability. How could she tell the nominating committee No? But she did. She had to say No to people in order to say Yes to God. And He has blessed her ministry and opened doors for her—doors that may seem scary and overwhelming but that have also been exciting. I'm excited for her.

Lilly and I have chatted by e-mail and in person about balance in our lives—trying to figure out how to know exactly what it is God wants us to do. She knew I was working on a book about balance and asked, "How can you write a book about something you're attempting to find in your own life? If you haven't arrived, how can you be credible?"

Good question—and one I've asked myself as I've written and thought and prayed. I know I haven't found lasting balance in every area of my life. I know that doing so may be a struggle I face all my life. But God has taught me much.

He has shown me that He does have a purpose for my life. That purpose is knowing Him. Knowing God has to be a priority in my life. He has also given me a ministry. He gives each of us a ministry; we just may not realize it yet—or know what a ministry looks like. We may think a ministry means traveling, speaking, or giving Bible studies. But ministry means using the gifts and talents and abilities God has given us to make a difference in the lives of those He has placed in our path. Our ministry may change as our lives grow and change. When my children were young, they were my ministry. They still are, but as they grow, God has opened up more opportunities for me. Tim's ministry is being available to the people at his work—living the life of a Christian before men and women who never go to church. They may know God's name only as a swear word, but they watch Tim every day. Sue's ministry is listening to hurting people and training others how to listen and help.

I've learned that I don't have to do it all. I have to do only what God has asked. People will ask me to do a lot of things—good things—that God has not given me to do. So if I truly desire to have time to do what He wants, I have to say No. I may disappoint people. I may have to say No to things that no one else will do. People may not understand, but that is OK. God understands, and that is what matters. I'm learning to do the truly important and to let go of what is only urgent. Some things can wait. I'm choosing to do what matters most, not what is screaming most for attention.

Some decisions are simple. On Monday evening, Tim and I were supposed to attend our church board meeting where I was scheduled to make a presentation. But Tim was working late because of the accident at his company. He didn't know when he would get home. I knew that after such a tough day, he would need me to be there, to listen, and to hold him. (At least I hoped that he would need me.) So I skipped the board meeting. Being a wife is more important to me than being a member of the church board. Someone else was able to fill in for me. When Tim got home, I knew I had made the right decision.

I may have to choose what comes first—take the boys to ride go-carts or clean the house? The answer may be different at different times. Life is full of choices. I need to think, "What is really important to me?" and then make that my priority; even if it isn't what others may think is important.

I've made a list of all my roles and responsibilities. I've listed them in order of their priority to me. I pray through this list regularly. And I try to make sure that those things that are most important to me get the biggest part of my schedule, which has too often been eaten up by little things that really don't matter that much. Now my priorities fill my calendar.

Taking time for myself has become one of those priorities, taking the time to grow in my relationship with God. I'm not talking about keeping up with a to-do list for devotional time but getting to know God better through prayer, Bible study, music, nature, and worship. I'm exercising and eating healthy. I'm spending time with friends and family. I'm carving out some uninterrupted time to read or listen to music. I'm taking a day off now and then to do something fun, to relax. I'm scheduling time to do the things I feel called to do—like writing.

There are days when priorities conflict. I may want to spend time with friends, but there is a project demanding to be done. In those cases, the most urgent takes over. The project gets done. But I reward myself with some "friend time" later.

My days aren't carefree and simple. They are still busy. They probably always will be. Sometimes I think I thrive on being busy. For me, finding balance will never mean day after day of nothing to do, no demands, no trials. Trials and busyness will always be a part of my life—of the life of each of us. The balance comes in how I handle it all. Whether the to-do list or God becomes my focus. Whether I spend all my time doing things or doing what is truly important. Balance comes when I stand still and allow God to work instead of trying to fix it myself. When I trust Him instead of worrying and being afraid—and live out that trust in my actions.

In *God's Joyful Surprise*, Sue Monk Kidd comes to the same conclusion—that we need God to be at the center of everything. He needs to be our focus, our "center" as she calls Him. She writes,

> Yes, that's what we need. But I don't think for a minute that a centered life is the solution to all our problems. Rather it is a way to respond to our problems. We don't withdraw from the world to a center. We respond to the world from our center.
>
> Instead of rushing about, accepting every job that comes, we get a sense of what's really important. Being centered allows us to bring that elusive quality of focus to our lives. It enables us to set priorities. From the center we can respond to the chaos by eliminating that which isn't meaningful and bringing order and calm to the rest. For in the center we are rooted in God's love. In such a place there is no need for

striving and impatience and dashing about seeking approval.

We need not avoid our active lives, but simply bring to them a new vision and shift of gravity. We are called to live a life rich and full, but rooted firmly in the center where all is drawn together in God and then flows out of His presence. That is when life becomes the silent dance revolving around Him, alive with the music of His love.

With God as our focus or center, our lives will still be busy, but they will be busy *with* Him—not *for* Him or *in spite of* Him, but *with* Him. He will be our reason for the things we do. Not the approval of someone else. Not because no one else will do it. Not because it has to be done. But because He has called us to do it. Whatever it is He calls us to do—whether it be to wipe runny noses, type reports for our bosses, or wait on that impossible customer with grace and kindness—He calls us to rest in Him and for Him. He calls us to find balance in Him alone.

Thinking and Talking About It

1. Which sister best describes you—Martha or Mary?

2. What things most distract you from the truly important?

3. What have you learned that can help you to let go of distractions and focus on what is truly important?

4. What are the most important things in your life? What are the things that define your life—that make you who you are?

5. How can you avoid getting caught up in the urgent and instead, live your life focused on the priorities?

If you enjoyed this book, you'll enjoy these as well:

The Gift of Friendship
Tamyra Horst. God has created within each of us a desire to connect with others, a need for someone to talk to and share our hopes and dreams with. That's what friends are for, and in this book, Tamyra Horst unwraps God's gift of friendship—how to make, keep, and nurture friends.
0-8163-1709-7. Paperback. US$8.99, Cdn$12.99.

Gathering
Sandra Doran and *Dale Slongwhite.* Two sisters seek to show that life is more than a vertical climb toward career success. Through personal and shared experiences, the authors help us find balance and fulfillment in the numerous tangible and intangible bits of life we gather as we journey through this world.
0-8163-1696-1. Paperback. US$10.99, Cdn$15.99.

Slow Down and Simplify
Beverly Graham Stickle. Tips and advice from those who've learned how to simplify finances, shopping, schedules, cooking, gift giving, child care, pet care—and much, much more. Also contains a special chapter on being involved in church while still having time left over!
0-8163-1688-0. US$10.99, Cdn$15.99.

Order from your ABC by calling **1-800-765-6955**, or get online and shop our virtual store at **www.adventistbookcenter.com**.
- Read a chapter from your favorite book
- Order online
- Sign up for e-mail notices on new products